ALSO BY MARVIN E. FRANKEL

Criminal Sentences: Law Without Order (1973)

The Grand Jury—An Institution on Trial (1977)
(with Gary P. Naftalis)

Partisan Justice (1980)

Out of the Shadows of Night:
The Struggle for International Human Rights (1989)
(with Ellen Saideman)

FAITH AND FREEDOM

Faith
and
Freedom

RELIGIOUS LIBERTY IN AMERICA

Marvin E. Frankel

A CRITICAL ISSUE

CONSULTING EDITOR: ERIC FONER

HILL AND WANG • NEW YORK
A division of Farrar, Straus and Giroux

Copyright © 1994 by Marvin E. Frankel
All rights reserved
Printed in the United States of America
Published simultaneously in Canada by HarperCollins*CanadaLtd*
First edition, 1994

LIBRARY OF CONGRESS CATALOGING-IN-PUBLICATION DATA
Frankel, Marvin E.
Faith and freedom : religious liberty in America / Marvin E.
Frankel. — 1st ed.
p.   cm. — (A Critical issue)
Includes bibliographical references and index.
1. Freedom of religion—United States.   2. Church and state—
United States.   3. United States—Constitutional law—
Amendments—1st.   I. Title.   II. Series.
KF4783.F7   1994
342.73'0852—dc20   [347.302852]   94-13418 CIP

For Alice, of course

CONTENTS

FAITH AND FREEDOM

INTRODUCTION

Hᴵɢʜ among the "blessings of liberty" for which American colonists dared the Atlantic and then adopted the Constitution was the ideal of religious liberty. With some lapses and wrong turns that go with the human condition, our approach to the ideal has been close—close enough to be gratifying even for nonchauvinist Americans.

Like other historical complexities, the relationship, including the separation, between church and state in America results from a variety of factors—among others, the goals of the early settlers, the multiplicity of sects and the absence of a dominant majority, the frontiersman's preference for being left alone, and, not least, the influence of Enlightenment philosophy. Thus, although the central statement is in the Religion Clauses of the Constitution's First Amendment, the roots are far wider and deeper than the strictly legal or political factors. The keen-eyed observer Tocqueville noticed before the middle of the nineteenth century that Americans of diverse religions had contrived to live together without adopting Europeans' habits of killing or abusing each other on account of their religious differences. He did not find it necessary or relevant to rely on the American Constitution to explain that, and it would not have been especially relevant then, since, as we'll note again, the Religion Clauses of the First Amendment applied until around 1940 only to the federal government and not to the states.

As we've moved through the second half of the twentieth century, however, the uniquely American character of religious freedom—including equal respect not only for the varying religions but for the choice to accept no formal religion at all—has been sustained to a large degree by our constitutional law. This is particularly true, essentially by definition, of this book's subject, the relationship between government on one hand and matters of religious faith and functioning on the other. The subject has come to seem at times remarkably subtle and perplexing. The resulting divisions on the Supreme Court have often been close and the differing opinions testy. For all that, though, the simply stated ideal remains unchanged: freedom of conscience for everyone in this polyglot community.

Believing it valuable to understand the major conflicts and understandings about religion and public power, I've tried in this short essay to sketch the leading issues by examining some of the major court arguments in which they have emerged. The result, like the subject, remains controversial. So I declare at the outset my view that separation of church and state—keeping each free of the power of the other—has been a vital principle of our well-being. Acknowledging that there are no absolutes in the law, I do not argue for total or hermetic separation. But my position comes fairly close to that. Several of the decisions I regard as mistakes are cases where the Supreme Court has allowed religious groups or symbols to become identified with the power of the state.

The still higher vital principle, for which church-state separation serves as an essential means, is the ultimate goal stated at the outset—the freedom to exercise or to refrain from exercising any religion. Congratulating us, as I have, on that, I'll indicate some of the imperfections and the ever-present dangers.

I should concede explicitly that 100 pages or so are not enough for a fully rounded and impartial account. I'm not neutral on the subject of this book. For a somewhat tendentious analogy from another segment of the First Amendment, I'm not neutral about free speech either. The purpose of this writing is to describe bedrock principles as they have been bodied forth in dramatic controversies, and to lend modest support to those principles as I see them.

A final, apologetic note. The pages that follow are peppered with footnote symbols. Most readers should feel comfortable ignoring them. They are merely citations to cases and books. They reflect, beyond a degree of pedantry, a concern for the reader who may want to pursue the subject further.

1

GREAT WORDS,
CLOSE QUESTIONS

T HE first sixteen words of the First Amendment to the U.S. Constitution, the beginning of the Bill of Rights, are these:

> Congress shall make no law respecting an establishment of
> religion, or prohibiting the free exercise thereof.

The fact that they come first need not signify their firstness in importance. The framers may or may not—or some may and others may not—have deemed them the most precious of the protected rights. It is enough for present, or any, purposes that the words embody values at the heart of the understandings on which diverse Americans live at peace with one another. This is in any event a central thesis of my book.

The thesis may seem questionable when we recall that 150, 200, and more years after the First Amendment was adopted, the Justices of the Supreme Court have continued to divide as closely as 5–4 over what it means. I think there is no contradiction, however, and I mean in the course of these pages to show why. It helps set the scene for that and other arguments to look at some of the 5–4 cases and see what divides the Justices and others.

In the wake of World War II, when questions long hushed broke through former fears and inhibitions, the Supreme Court decided *Everson v. Board of Education*,[1] what lawyers call a "leading case." The question was whether the school board was violating the Establishment Clause ("no law respecting an establishment of religion") by using public money to pay for transporting young students to parochial schools. Taxpayer Everson—joined by Seventh-Day Adventists, the American Civil Liberties Union, and a Council of the United American Mechanics of New Jersey—had sued to bar that assistance. Justice Hugo Black, writing for the majority, drew on Thomas Jefferson and others to declare that the Establishment Clause erected a "wall of separation" between church and state. The position, steadily quoted and still debated, was put this way:

> The "establishment of religion" clause of the First Amendment means at least this: Neither a state nor the Federal Government can set up a church. Neither can pass laws which aid one religion, aid all religions, or prefer one religion over another. Neither can force nor influence a person to go to or to remain away from church against his will or force him to profess a belief or disbelief in any religion. No person can be punished for entertaining or professing religious beliefs or disbeliefs, for church attendance or non-attendance. No tax in any amount, large or small, can be levied to support any religious activities or institutions, whatever they may be called, or whatever form they may adopt to teach or practice religion. Neither a state nor the Federal government can, openly or secretly, partic-

ipate in the affairs of any religious organizations or groups and vice versa. In the words of Jefferson, the clause against establishment of religion by law was intended to erect "a wall of separation between church and State."

On those premises all nine Justices agreed—and this remains settled law—that government money may not be used to support religious schools or institutions, "whatever they may be called."[2] On the other hand, it seemed also to be agreed that "general welfare" benefits could not be withheld from parochial-school children—for instance, the services of state-paid policemen at school crossings, fire protection, sewage disposal, and so forth. As the majority put it, and nobody disagreed, the First Amendment requires the state to be "neutral" as between believers and non-believers, but certainly does not command the state to be their "adversary."

With the issue thus framed, the majority found it a suitable "general welfare" concern that parents should have safe transport to school for their children. Characterizing the decision for the school board, Justice Black wrote:

> The First Amendment has erected a wall between church and state. That wall must be kept high and impregnable. We could not approve the slightest breach. New Jersey has not breached it here.[3]

In a Court largely characterized as "New Deal" and "liberal" (and including former Republican Senator Harold Burton in the dissent), there were two vigorous dissenting opinions for the minority of four. Justice Robert Jackson found the actual decision "discordant" with the broadly stated wall-of-separation principle. It recalled Byron's Julia, he said, who, "whispering 'I will ne'er consent' consented.[4] Catholic education, he wrote, "is the rock on which" the

Catholic Church is founded, and aid to the school is not different from aid to the Church itself.[5]

Justice Wiley Rutledge found "corrosive" this first "square" decision on the Establishment Clause and deemed it a first breach in the wall of separation. He pointed out that the clause forbade not only "an established church, but any law respecting an establishment of religion."[6] The separation of church and state was to be "complete and permanent."[7] He recalled James Madison's leadership, first in Virginia, then in the national Constitutional Convention, against any semblance of tax support (not even "three pence only") for religious institutions. Religion, he said, was constitutionally "a private affair" that the state could neither restrain nor assist. He found unpersuasive the general public availability of police and fire protection. Public money that effectively aided parochial education would bring "the struggle of sect against sect for the larger share or for any."[8] He opposed the majority result as inconsistent with Madison's aim "to keep separate the separate spheres [of church and state] as the First Amendment drew them; to prevent the first experiment upon our liberties; and to keep the question from becoming entangled in corrosive precedents."[9]

Looking back fifty years or so, the Court's division in 1947 may seem to have been expressed in excessively sharp terms. But the disagreement was not unimportant; it is a key task of the Justices to note even slight tilts one way or another that may define wide gulfs as the lines extend in time. Nevertheless, the case stands after all as a landmark for what was unanimous rather than a harbinger of grave divergences. What remains as its prime consequence is the broad agreement on bedrock principles, not the dispute on applying the principles to the particular issue of school transportation. The unanimous recognition of the "wall of separation" as a key structure in church-state relations reaffirmed Thomas Jefferson's dictum in powerful terms. It remains a live and invaluable premise for keeping the hands of the governors and the clerics off each other's domains. Still, Justices and others down to this day hack at the wall and carp at the expression as a "mere metaphor." But more than a figure of speech is at stake. The continuing debate, if it does not threaten the central premises of the Religion Clauses, has ongoing consequences for the sometimes wavy lines the courts draw in treating the steady stream of disputes. We'll be returning to this.

This is not meant to be a technical legal text. However, a couple of other close cases will help to identify some of the problems and conflicting interests that flow through the court-houses. While the phraseology changes, the notion of *separation* remains a key idea.

In 1992 the case of *Lee v. Weisman* again divided the Court 5–4, this time over a "non-sectarian" prayer (the quotation marks identify a solemnly intoned "Judeo-Christian" expression that is an oxymoron to the ears of Buddhists, atheists, and others who are sectarian nonprayers) at a high-school graduation exercise. Daniel Weisman and his daughter, the graduate, sued to block any prayer at her graduation as a violation of the First Amendment. The principal overrode their protests, and a rabbi came to deliver the graduation prayer. By a one-vote margin, the High Court held this unconstitutional.

In the majority opinion for the Court, despite the close vote, Justice Anthony Kennedy said there was no need to struggle again with tough questions that had been dividing the bench for some years. It was enough, he wrote, that the school-promoted prayer manifested a "pervasive" involve-ment with a religious exercise, down to supplying the rabbi with a set of "Guidelines for Civic Occasions." The result was that the exercise engendered the kind of divisiveness and "social pressure" to conform that amounted to "coercion" of those for whom the prayer was an objectionable exercise. He reaffirmed that under the First Amendment religious beliefs are "too precious to be either proscribed or prescribed by the State."

Two concurring opinions recalled that under the precedents coercion was sufficient but not necessary to violate the Establishment Clause. Justice David Souter also stressed the Court's repeated pronouncements that the First Amendment forbids not only discrimination between religions but also discrimination between religion and nonreligion—a point on which he noted that Chief Justice William Rehnquist and others took a minority, dissenting view.

Justice Antonin Scalia—joined by three others—wrote the kind of nasty dissent that has become his hallmark, at odds though it may be with the kind of Olympian dialogue we would wish to associate with the Supreme Court. He ridiculed the majority's perception of coercion, finding the Kennedy opinion a "psycho-journey" arriving at a "psycho-coercion test." He found the Court majority's concern for the sensibilities of "nonbelievers" an unrealistic, unfounded sentimentalism, observing that any psychic strain on nonbelievers was imaginary, or trivial at worst. He stressed the importance of ceremonial prayer to most Americans and found detestable the conclusion that this value should be obstructed by dissident groups or individuals. He regretted angrily that the "simple and inspiring prayers of Rabbi Gutterman" at the graduation ceremony should have been found violative of the Constitution.

Justice Scalia's dissent, garnering four votes at the end of the Reagan-Bush years, stands a good chance of being the high-water mark of the minority attempt to extinguish ideas of separation and government neutrality that the Court had enforced with only occasional slippage since 1947. In both style and substance, the opinion exhibits an impatient distaste for deviant sensibilities getting in the way of majority preferences—which is, very broadly speaking, what the First Amendment is for.

The dissent finds in the Court decision a "bulldozer of . . . social engineering," using as "its instrument of destruction . . . a boundless, and boundlessly manipulable, test of psychological coercion." Graduation prayers are an old tradition, Scalia writes, and the majority's idea of "coercion" leads him to observe that "interior decorating is a rock-hard science compared to psychology practiced by amateurs." There is no coercion, he declares, in having it a condition of attendance at the graduation that students stand or maintain a "respectful silence" for prayers that they find objectionable or offensive as a matter of conscience. Nobody is forced to do these things, he says, and that should be the end of it. One wonders how he would deal with the case on some later or different day when the great majority of the students, willingly and uncoerced, were on their knees, with or without foreheads touching the floor, during the ceremonial prayer. In any event, the Justice says, "coercion" historically meant legal compulsion to religious orthodoxy, not the kind of peer pressure the majority finds significant.

Approaching his conclusion, Justice Scalia trivializes what the Court decides by explaining how the ruling may be avoided:

> Given the odd basis for the court's decision, invocations and benedictions will be able to be given at public-school graduations next June, as they have for the past century and a half, so long as school authorities make clear that anyone who abstains from screaming in protest does not necessarily participate in the prayers. All that is seemingly needed is an announcement, or perhaps a written insertion at the beginning of the graduation Program, to the effect that, while all are asked to rise for the invocation and benediction, none is compelled to join in them, nor will be assumed, by rising, to have done so. That obvious fact recited, the graduates and their parents may proceed to thank God,

as Americans have always done, for the blessings He has generously bestowed on them and on their country.[10]

Continuing in that religious vein, which expresses his own sentiments (probably shared by a majority of Americans), Justice Scalia observes that nothing "is so inclined to foster among religious believers of various faiths a toleration—no, an affection—for one another than voluntarily joining in prayer together, to the God whom they all worship and seek." Overlooking the 10–12 percent of the population who profess no religion, and the various religions that do not recognize his one God, Justice Scalia says a Baptist or Catholic would be "inoculated from religious bigotry and prejudice in a manner that cannot be replicated" if he or she "heard and joined in the simple and inspiring prayers" of the rabbi at that graduation ceremony.

Those devout expressions are, I've suggested, the last gasp in the twentieth century of a position that would mingle government and religion, as the dissenting opinion does. The majority of the Court might share, but refrains from expressing, the view that the rabbi's prayers were "inspiring." Others may not. Every reader may judge what inspired Justice Scalia by reading it:

God of the Free, Hope of the Brave
For the legacy of America where diversity is celebrated and the rights of minorities are protected, we thank You. May these young men and women grow up to enrich it.
For the liberty of America, we thank You. May these new graduates grow up to guard it.
For the political process of America in which all its citizens may participate, for its court system where all may seek justice we thank You. May those we honor this morning always turn to it in trust.
For the destiny of America we thank You. May the grad-

uates of Nathan Bishop Middle School so live that they
might help to share it.

May our aspirations for our country and for these young
people, who are our hope for the future, be richly fulfilled.

Those words, found "inspiring" by Justice Scalia, may seem
banal or even offensive to others for purposes of graduation
exercises. That is not in itself significant. What is of some
consequence is that the Justice, a public official, should find
it appropriate to declare in an official pronouncement whether
a religious expression is "inspiring" or not. This is a small
clue to a larger attitude—an attitude that permeates the minority opinion and is notably eschewed by the majority.

The majority opinion, if I've left any slight doubt about
this, is the one I espouse. Much of what is written in later
chapters reflects, and will try to support, this position—
namely, as Roger Williams had it three centuries ago, that
there must be a sharp line between the garden and the wilderness, the "garden" being the realm of the spirit and the
"wilderness" that of secular governmental authority. Before
proceeding to some of the history and the arguments, one
more close question is a useful item for an opening chapter.

Lynch v. Donnelly (1984)[11] is one of several cases in which
the Supreme Court has considered crèches and other religious
symbols displayed by public officials or others in public places.
That suit involved a long-standing tradition in Pawtucket,
Rhode Island, of displaying a crèche owned by the city in a
park owned by a nonprofit organization in the heart of the
shopping district. Donnelly and others, members of a local
affiliate of the American Civil Liberties Union, along with the
affiliate, sued in federal court to bar the display. They won
in the trial court and the court of appeals, but the Supreme
Court reversed 5–4.

The majority opinion, by Chief Justice Warren Burger, said
that the metaphor of the wall of separation had never meant

total separation of church and state, noted that Christmas is a national holiday, acknowledged that the recognition of "Christ's Mass" and the crèche as its symbol were "identified with one religious faith" (p. 685), but declared that forbidding the public display "would be a stilted overreaction" (p. 686). In passages that were to be further debated later on, he stated that the crèche did not stand alone but was part of a display that included a Santa Claus house, reindeer, a Christmas tree, and other nonreligious figures.

Justice Sandra O'Connor, concurring with the majority in a separate opinion that has had continuing weight, said Establishment Clause violations should be found where government "entangles" itself unduly with religion or expresses "endorsement or disapproval," sending "a message to nonadherents that they are outsiders, not full members of the political community, and an accompanying message to adherents that they are insiders, favored members of the political community" (p. 688). Some scholarly commentators (and I) found her words and her vote for the crèche difficult to reconcile.

Justice William Brennan (along with Justices Thurgood Marshall, Harry Blackmun, and John Stevens) dissented. He found the Establishment Clause violated by a symbol selected to "Keep Christ in Christmas," pitching the prestige of government on the side of the Christian majority, while inflicting "an insult and injury" on non-Christians, including Jews, believers in other religions, and those adhering to no religion at all.

While the Supreme Court is the final authority in any given case, a vote of 5 to 4 suggests the possibility that more may yet be heard on the particular subject. That has been true of government funds spent for parochial-school children and for crèches and other religious symbols in public places. It is likely to be true for prayers in public-school settings. What these sharp divisions mean or ought to mean for us is a topic that will recur as we go along. At this juncture, a 1989 sequel to the crèche case, with the addition of a menorah, is an interesting illustration of how close and difficult—some say tortured—these problems can become.

The first paragraph of the decision makes that point in a schematic fashion:

> JUSTICE BLACKMUN announced the judgment of the Court and delivered the opinion of the Court with respect to Parts III-A, IV, and V, an opinion with respect to Parts I and II, in which JUSTICE STEVENS and JUSTICE O'CONNOR join, an opinion with respect to Part III-B, in which JUSTICE STEVENS joins, an opinion with respect to Part VII, in which JUSTICE O'CONNOR joins, and an opinion with respect to Part VI.

Justice Blackmun wrote the first and main opinion, but neither he nor anyone else had contrived an *opinion* that mustered five votes. To put it more sharply, the opinion as a whole did not win even another vote. As for the *judgment*, which is the governing result reached by the Court, that gets put together by a complex scorecard of partial concurrences and dissents. What could so fracture the views of the nine jurists?

The subject was an annual display on public property in Pittsburgh—a crèche on the Grand Staircase of the Allegheny County Courthouse and a Hanukkah menorah outside the City-County Building "next to a Christmas tree and a sign saluting liberty." "No figures of Santa Claus or other decoration appeared on the Grand Staircase" along with the crèche (580–81). In an array of five opinions covering 100 pages, the Court split 5–4 in finding the crèche a violation of the Establishment Clause and 6–4 in allowing the menorah. The crèche was unacceptable, the majority held, because unlike the one in Pawtucket (the *Lynch v. Donnelly* case), this one stood in isolation (no Santa Claus, reindeer, etc.) in a splendid hall, and in other respects conveyed an "endorsement" of

Christian faith. Four dissenters, in an opinion by Justice Kennedy, found the focus on details a trivialization of the Constitution, a "jurisprudence of minutiae" relying on little more than "intuition and a tape measure."

The six voting to allow the menorah went on a scattering of ideas. Among others, as Justice Blackmun stressed, was the thought that the juxtaposition of the Christmas tree (nonreligious) and the sign celebrating liberty made the symbolic acknowledgment of Hanukkah a secular celebration of the season, not a display that viewers might see as endorsing or favoring the Jewish religion. The three who would have barred the menorah as well as the crèche worried lest this decision might lead laypeople unfamiliar with First Amendment mysteries to find favoritism being displayed toward Judaism. The four who would have upheld the crèche as well as the menorah objected that the favorable result for the Jewish symbol could mean that the "largest" religions are now to be made the "least favored faiths so as to avoid any possible risk of offending members of minority religions" (p. 677).

That is a very broad summary of 100 pages of sometimes intricate, often vitriolic judicial prose. It is enough, I think, for these introductory, scene-setting pages. I want to say at the outset that for all the seemingly hairline distinctions and bitter rhetoric, the Supreme Court's jurisprudence on the Religion Clauses has on the whole served the nation admirably in the twentieth century. The cases are close because the questions that reach the Supreme Court are exquisitely difficult. The seeming attention to minutiae, with all respect to Justice Kennedy, reflects an honored and familiar task of trying to find sensible lines of distinction at the margins. This has been the way common-law judges have struggled over the centuries with all manner of hard cases—groping and even vacillating while they try, not always succeeding, to find clear and agreed doctrine.

With the garden and the wilderness, there is a recurrent

and endless job of edging to be done. Single cases may lead to finicky, seemingly hair-splitting decisions. The shift of a vote or the replacement of a Justice may make all the difference. There is, viewing the picture close up, an appearance of petty squabbling and arbitrary rulings.

At a little distance, the work of the Court (leaving aside some of the regrettable tone) is more to be admired and appreciated. The high value of mutual forbearance in a community of numerous divisions has been well served. The pressures to dismantle the wall of separation and to rein in the unorthodox beat unrelentingly on the courts and deliver a stream of challenges to Washington. The responses, if they satisfy no one all the time, have contributed vitally to the health of a free and open society.

The story is less bright when we turn to the other branches of government and to activist forces in the community against which the First Amendment was drawn to safeguard. Many of the quandaries that emerge in the docket of the Supreme Court arrive there because resolute people, for reasons that are sometimes good and sometimes not, are determined to test and if possible change the boundaries marked by the First Amendment. No matter how many times the Court forbids public support of parochial schools, parents and church leaders will respond incredulously to the law's requirement that they pay taxes for public schools while they also pay tuition for private schools. No matter how many private crèches or menorahs can reside in private places, including prominently visible places, proponents will insist on public displays, lit or tarnished by the aura of government, while insisting this does nothing to indicate governmental endorsement or sponsorship. The Supreme Court can speak all it likes against prayers sponsored by public authorities; still, in athletic stadiums across the land tax-paid principals and coaches will feel the contest can't be risked without a pre-game huddle for an explicitly Christian prayer, notwithstanding the different religions or nonreligion of a few players and people in the stands.

The principals and coaches, and other more prominent public figures, are a main concern. Samuel Johnson spoke of patriotism as the last refuge of scoundrels. He might as well or better have said it of religion. Few things have sold better on the hustings than denouncing the Supreme Court for "expelling God" from the public schools. Instead of rallying to the Court's defense, legislators and other devout candidates have led the cries of anguish, never stopping to ask whether the spiritual health of the people is nurtured by the banalities that pass for prayer in the schools. Hypocrisy has never seemed a large price to pay for votes. It is not easy to quantify, but experience teaches that many of God's pols have no longer-range view of salvation than the results of the next election. President John Kennedy, our first and thus far only Roman Catholic President, was a notable exception. When Catholic clergymen were among the many, along with hordes of politicians, cursing out the Supreme Court for its 1962 decision invalidating a school prayer composed (believe it or not) by New York's Board of Regents, his was a calmer voice:

> [T]he Supreme Court has made its judgment and a good many people obviously will disagree with it. Others will agree with it. But I think that it is important for us if we are going to maintain our constitutional principle that we support the Supreme Court decisions even when we may not agree with them.
>
> In addition, we have in this case a very easy remedy and that is to pray ourselves. And I would think that it would be a welcome reminder to every American family that we can pray a good deal more at home, we can attend our churches with a good deal more fidelity, and we can make the true meaning of prayer much more important in the lives of all of our children. That power is very much open to us. And I would hope that as a result of this decision

that all American parents will intensify their efforts at home, and the rest of us will support the Constitution and the responsibility of the Supreme Court in interpreting it, which is theirs, and given to them by the Constitution.[13]

A major—*the* major—theme of this book is support of the position succinctly stated by John Kennedy. What he said in less metaphoric terms fairly and sensibly echoed Thomas Jefferson's plea for a wall of separation between church and state. Both saw, one at the beginning and the other after nearly 200 years of experience, that the coercive mingling of God's and Caesar's commands could lead to nothing but trouble for a society of diverse beliefs about ultimate things. The prudent advice they gave continues to be embattled—opposed by sincere bigots, by opportunist hucksters, and by those whose faith is too weak to tolerate the threat of different convictions.

I propose to illustrate and to argue that the wall of separation has been a treasure for the polyglot American family. The opponents of the principle—those who seek the clout of government to back their religious beliefs—base themselves, I think, on erroneous views of history and of true religious devotion. In a long, prudent perspective, it can be seen that they risk freedom of religion for themselves as well as others. This was understood by the framers of the Bill of Rights, whose good work is recalled in the next chapter. I propose then to review the varieties of efforts to impair that work—never with great success, but always threatening a cornerstone of our democratic freedoms.

2

GENESIS OF THE
RELIGION CLAUSES:
HISTORY AND LUCKY
STARS

JUSTICE Hugo Black's opinion in the school transportation case (*Everson*) is again a good starting point. He recalled there in brief summary the centuries of religious persecution and bloodshed that had preceded the American colonial experience, setting the scene for the First Amendment guarantees as safeguards against recurrences:

A large proportion of the early settlers of this country came here from Europe to escape the bondage of laws which compelled them to support and attend government-favored churches. The centuries immediately before and contemporaneous with the colonization of America had been filled with turmoil, civil strife, and persecutions, generated in large part by established sects determined to maintain their absolute political and religious supremacy. With the power of government supporting them, at various times and places, Catholics had persecuted Protestants, Protestants had persecuted Catholics, Protestant sects had persecuted other Protestant sects, Catholics of one shade of belief had persecuted Catholics of another shade of belief, and all of these had from time to time persecuted Jews. In efforts to force loyalty to whatever religious group happened to be on top and in league with the government of a particular time and place, men and women had been fined, cast in jail, cruelly tortured, and killed. Among the offenses for which these punishments had been inflicted were such things as speaking disrespectfully of the views of ministers of government-established churches, non-attendance at those churches, expressions of non-belief in their doctrines and failure to pay taxes and tithes to support them.

That was a large piece of the story, but by no means the whole. If we were consistently rational and foresighted, the prior experience of the American colonists would have been enough to establish religious freedom and disestablish churches once and for all after their arrival here. If we are "consistently" anything, however, it is not rational and foresighted. Predictably, the settlers demonstrated on a large scale that the basic aversion was not against religious oppression in principle but against being at the victimized end of oppression. Having fled from established churches they opposed, the new Americans proceeded in most of the colonies to establish churches of their own preference. As Justice Black went on to write:

The[ ] practices of the old world were transplanted to and began to thrive in the soil of the new America. The very charters granted by the English Crown to the individuals and companies designated to make the laws which would control the destinies of the colonials authorized these individuals and companies to erect religious establishments which all, whether believers or nonbelievers, would be required to support and attend. An exercise of this authority was accompanied by a repetition of many of the old-world practices and persecutions. Catholics found themselves hounded and proscribed because of their faith; Quakers who followed their conscience went to jail; Baptists were peculiarly obnoxious to certain dominant Protestant sects; men and women of varied faiths who happened to be in a minority in a particular locality were persecuted because they steadfastly persisted in worshipping God only as their own consciences dictated. And all of these dissenters were compelled to pay tithes and taxes to support government-sponsored churches whose ministers preached inflammatory sermons designed to strengthen and consolidate the established faith by generating a burning hatred against dissenters.

Basically, then, the regimes of almost all the colonies enthroned strictly defined Protestant orthodoxies and called upon everyone for material support and overt respect for the religious establishments. As Justice Black said, the disfavored minorities included deviant Protestants as well as the more heretical Roman Catholics and Jews. Peter Stuyvesant was harsh and hostile not only to Jews but to Lutherans and Quakers as well. The bitter experiences of Roger Williams and Anne Hutchinson illustrate the tight controls. The burned witches of Salem in 1691 recall the depths of the horrors thought to be God's requirements.

There were exceptions. Banished from Massachusetts by the Puritans, Roger Williams founded a religiously tolerant society in Rhode Island that for a long while remained far ahead of its time (and actually did some backsliding after the death of Williams). William Penn's colony is remembered as a similarly benign place, putting to one side such qualifications as the fact that Jews could not hold office, and atheists and deists were forbidden even to live in the colony. On the whole, in any event, without pursuing its details, which are fully related elsewhere, we know that liberty of conscience—even the freedom not to show up in church—was scarcely the order of life in colonial America.

Before we turn our anachronistic scorn on those spiritual ancestors, it pays to remember that mutual tolerance of religious differences has never been, and is not to this day, the characteristic stance of humankind. We all hate to be subordinated and oppressed for our deep beliefs, which largely define for us who and what we are. Notwithstanding that, it is by no means "natural" or instinctive, despite the scriptural admonitions about dealing with our neighbors, to recognize and respect these sentiments in others who disagree with us and therefore live in error—or, worse, sin. So the victims and outcasts adapt readily, when the chance occurs, to the roles of victimizers and excluders.

The current state of religious affairs in Israel is a sad case in point. It might have been expected that a couple of millennia more or less as pariahs, bearing fresh memories of times when all were eligible for gas chambers without regard to precise religious or nonreligious preferences, would have led Jews to a position of the most unstinting mutual tolerance. This expectation, if anyone had it, has not been met. While it is not their primary preoccupation, bitter religious differences are vividly manifested in the daily lives of Israeli Jews. As described by one sympathetic scholar, the disagreements are not expressed in uniformly peaceable forms:

> Ultra-Orthodox Jews have, *inter alia*, vandalized bus shelters which display advertisements they consider lewd and licentious; thrown rocks at cars traveling on the Sabbath and protested the showing of films on the Sabbath eve; desecrated the tombstones of former governmental leaders in protest against archaeological excavations on allegedly sacred ground; sent threatening letters to hospitals perform-

ing heart and liver transplants, which they claim violate Jewish law; prevented groups of women from praying publicly and collectively at the Western Wall; and abruptly interrupted Reform religious services because women participated equally with men. In return, secularists have vandalized Orthodox synagogues and schools; protested religious privileges such as military deferments; and deliberately conducted motorcades near ultra-Orthodox neighborhoods on the Sabbath.[1]

Strife rather than forbearance has been the characteristic response to religious differences. How, then, did the United States get so lucky as to acquire the First Amendment? (Some will be offended, I realize, to hear of "luck" in connection with so providential a blessing. But I do believe, verily, that we are the beneficiaries of great good fortune in having a convergence of effective causes fall in place as they did. And resentment, at least here and there, goes with the territory in which this book ventures.) Approaching an answer to that question, let's begin by completing our hasty sketch of colonial history. As I've said, religious freedom in our contemporary understanding was not characteristic of those times. But the picture improved by the time of the Revolution and thereafter. Before the Revolution, except for Rhode Island, most of the future states continued to enforce Christianity in some measure or other, and all came close to that in requiring monotheistic beliefs and constraints. Five continued established churches. Georgia required all members of the legislature to "be of the Protestant religion." Most enforced Protestantism to some degree. By 1789, however, when the new Congress passed and proposed the Bill of Rights, the majority were ready to enact the Religion Clauses.

North Carolina had led the way. Along with evangelical Christians, Madison fought successfully in 1785–86 against a tax to support Christian churches. In one of the most famous documents of American history, his *Me-*

morial and Remonstrance Against Religious Assessments, addressed to the Virginia General Assembly in 1785, Madison attacked the renewal as a "dangerous abuse of power." Justifying the position, he wrote:

> The Religion . . . of every man must be left to the conviction and conscience of every man; and it is the right of every man to exercise it as these may dictate. This right is in its nature an unalienable right. It is unalienable . . . because the opinions of men, depending only on the evidence contemplated by their own minds, cannot follow the dictates of other men. . . . It is the duty of every man to render to the Creator such homage, and such only, as he believes to be acceptable to him.
>
> *   *   *
>
> Who does not see that the same authority which can establish Christianity, in exclusion of all other Religions, may establish with the same ease any particular sect of Christians, in exclusion of all other Sects? That the same authority which can force a citizen to contribute three pence only of his property for the support of any one establishment, may force him to conform to any other establishment in all cases whatsoever.
>
> *   *   *
>
> [T]he proposed establishment is a departure from that generous policy, which, offering asylum to the persecuted and oppressed of every Nation and Religion, promised a lustre to our country, and an accession to the number of its citizens. . . . Distant as it may be, in its present form, from the Inquisition it differs from it only in degree. The one is the first step, the other the last in the career of intolerance.
>
> *   *   *
>
> Torrents of blood have been spilt in the old world, by vain attempts of the secular arm to extinguish Religious discord, by proscribing all difference in Religious opinions. Time has at length revealed the true remedy.[2]

That "true remedy" was the defeat in Virginia of the law to tax people for the support of churches. The proposed law was resisted by Madison and Jefferson even though its supporters (including, prominently, Patrick Henry) sought to make it appealing by providing that taxpayers could choose the church their tax money would support, only provided that they chose *some* church.

Carrying the day against the Virginia proposal, Madison led again in the drafting and adoption of the First Amendment. Two centuries later, with some compromises and deviations here and there, the Supreme Court has taken up the leadership and remained essentially faithful to the teachings of Madison and Jefferson.

It is a vital part of even a thumbnail history to recall that the First Amendment as adopted limited only the *federal government*, not the states ("*Congress* shall make no law . . ."). It followed that for over a century and a half, the states were, so far as the federal Constitution was concerned, free to have established churches and to restrict religious freedom in ways not open to the national authorities. The power was disclaimed, however, by the states for themselves. All of them adopted close counterparts of the federal First Amendment. As a result, while several states continued taxing people to support church institutions until well into the nineteenth century (Massachusetts hanging on until 1833), the basic limits of the First Amendment were technically applicable to all levels of American government almost from the beginning.

Despite that general picture, the full-blown legal doctrine of church-state relations today is largely a twentieth-century development. The elaboration of First Amendment law, beginning after 1940, in cases like the three discussed in Chapter 1 and in a host of others, makes for a much more detailed, sophisticated, and effective jurisprudence than that evolved in the states for themselves. The springboard for the development was a ruling in 1940 that the post–Civil War Fourteenth Amendment, requiring due process in the states, "incorporated" the First Amendment Religion Clauses and made them applicable to the states. (Before and after 1940, the same idea of incorporation, still debated by some, was extended to most, though not all, of the Bill of Rights.) The result is that virtually all the major decisions on this subject, including those in Chapter 1, have involved questioned actions of state rather than federal officials. And most of the detailed meaning of the Religion Clauses has evolved through decisions since 1940.

This smattering of legal history grazes a large field of interest for lawyers and historians. Leaving all that for other settings, I want to pursue a broader aspect of the history: what, after all, explains why the American colonies and then the republic broke with the past and introduced to the world the ideas of church-state separation and religious freedom, with the freedom heavily dependent on the separation? Historic events like this do not have single, simple, or even thoroughly identifiable causes. Nevertheless, we surely know large pieces of the answer.

One factor, already mentioned, was the memory of less happy times and places. Obviously not decisive in itself, the desire to escape the combined grip of secular and religious control played a role.

In addition, relative indifference toward religion accounts in part for the willingness to tolerate diversity and the weakening of clerical authority. Whatever different speculations we might reach by guesswork, historians are agreed that church membership was proportionately much smaller two hundred years ago than it is today. It has been estimated that as few as one in eight people—or maybe even one in twenty or twenty-five—were church members in the colonies as against almost 64 percent in 1962 and a still higher percentage today.[3] That situation is reasonably inferred to show that people on the whole were probably less passionate either in supporting their own religious beliefs or in desiring to suppress the religious beliefs of others. As one twentieth-century scholar put it: "The indifferent man is tolerant of all religions because he lends his devotion to none."[4]

A broader, more positive way to put the same thought derives from the Bill of Rights as a whole. Those initial amendments to the Constitution reflected in diverse respects the increased emphasis on individual rights and the enlightened and caring attitudes toward fellow humans that had been growing during the seventeenth and eighteenth centuries. Across a considerable spectrum of relationships, the harsh cruelties of earlier times were giving way to respect, and the demand for respect, for the unique and variable individual. The portion of the First Amendment following the Religion Clauses proclaimed rights of free speech, press, and assembly, resting on the assumption that people the majority disliked would be unleashed to speak, write, and gather in support of their unorthodoxies. Accused criminals, notwithstanding the tendency to suppose that accusations signify guilt, were to have an array of safeguards. Searches and seizures were to be reasonable. Cruel and unusual punishments were forbidden. In the setting of these and other protections for the autonomous individual, freedom of conscience and the right to be different found readier acceptance than they had in earlier times.

In addition to the time, the place was favorable. While the predominant religion was Christianity, the colonies had received and coped variously with a number of divergent sects, often bitterly opposed to each other over differences that might look insignificant to non-Christians. The urge to dominate was steadily thwarted. The competition made liberty a practical and sensible alternative to continuous strife.

There were probably other causes. Some have suggested that persecution and intolerance were bad for business and came to be less acceptable in the wake of Adam Smith. If that is not a compelling explanation in light of the persistence of repression in most places, it may well have played a part in the new American world.

Whatever the exact causes and their weights, and with a

huge discount for the accepted sin of slavery, the blessings of liberty for the fortunate whites included the Constitution's promise of religious freedom, including the corollary resolve to keep religion and government out of each other's domain. The vital essence of those guarantees was and is the protection of minorities against majority control. That is thought by some to be anti-democratic, but the thought rests on an impoverished and simpleminded conception of democracy. If it was a novelty in the late eighteenth century, there is nothing strange any longer in the deeply civilized commitment of the majority to respect basic rights of minorities.

It has been said of this commitment that it is a "supreme form of generosity"—a right that "the majority concedes to minorities and hence . . . the noblest cry that has ever resounded in this planet."[5] That is true in a way and not a sentiment from which anyone would want to detract. At the same time, on a less romantic appraisal, the nobility of the majority is seen to be less completely self-denying. One of the surest limits on majorities is temporal. The fact that you are in a majority today—of Muslims, Republicans, or anything—is far from an assurance that the same group will be a majority tomorrow. As we've noted, the colonists had current evidence that they lived in a world of minorities. It was, then, as much a matter of prudence as generosity to erect safeguards against majority oppression.

This was a lively understanding for the framers of the Bill of Rights. It is lost recurrently in accesses of rage and impatience that regularly afflict majorities. It should never be lost for long enough to destroy the freedoms emplaced for all of us. This will be a basic premise here. As I've said already and will stress, the enemies of religious freedom, advertently or not, live with short horizons and an untutored notion of their own self-interest. This is a primary ground of the argument I'll be making for preservation of the wall of separation.

3

A CHRISTIAN—AT LEAST JUDEO-CHRISTIAN— NATION?

Historians and lawyers still debate whether the authors of the First Amendment intended government to stay neutral between religion and nonreligion, though a majority of the Supreme Court has ruled as of now that they did. Beyond debate, however, is that there was an intention to forbid favoring one or some religions over others. No religion was to receive support or favors from the government or to have a share in the powers of the state.

Notwithstanding that plain constitutional resolve, the position was not from the outset, and has never been, unanimous. Even as the First Amendment was being adopted, influential people hoped and worked for the day when the United States would affirm, frankly and explicitly, that the Christian religion of the majority at the creation was and is an official national creed. "From the beginning American Protestants entertained a lively hope that some day the civilization of the country would be fully Christian."[1] That hope has never died. There have been huge changes in the religious makeup as well as the size of the population. Protestants are no longer a majority; there is no majority. The aspirations of other sects have changed and grown as their numbers have grown. The essential Christian drive, in altered form, persists. "A once-powerful vision does not fade overnight; it continues to evoke expectations."[2]

Realistically, the Protestant hegemony existed as a matter of fact until only the other day as history goes, whatever the Constitution said. The fact that the overwhelming majority of Americans were Protestants made this in all probability inevitable. If most were not church members, their essential cultural qualities and habits were, in the now fading acronym, WASP (White Anglo-Saxon Protestant). More to the point, manifestations of Christian religiosity appeared on all kinds of public occasions almost, if not quite, as a matter of course. This condition continued from the first day, through the nineteenth century and well into the twentieth.

So, for example, the inauguration of President Washington featured Protestant church services among the official celebrations, notwithstanding the strict separationist views of Jefferson, Madison, and their contemporary adherents. Thanksgiving was from the outset declared and celebrated as a Christian holiday. The third and fourth Presidents, the very same Jefferson and Madison, opposed or abolished such official displays (and support) of the Christian faith, but their efforts were at best a temporary deviation. The first Congress opened its sessions with a Protestant chaplain's invocation. That practice continued until 1832, when the Senate elected a Roman Catholic priest as its chaplain. The departure in the direction of lower-case catholicity has never been permitted to run wild; neither house of Congress has ever had a Bahai, Buddhist, Islamic, Ethical Culture, or other fractional minority chaplain.

In the days when blasphemy could be punished as a state

crime (which is no longer true under the First Amendment's guarantee of free speech), the judges and others viewed this as a protection for the Christian faith, not for others. When the argument was made that if Christianity was thus defended, then blasphemy against other religions could also be made a crime, the answer was a brusque rejection. New York's Chancellor Kent, a leading jurist of the early nineteenth century, said the courts were not

> bound, by any expressions in the [state] constitution, as some have strangely supposed, either not to punish at all, or to punish indiscriminately the like attacks upon the religion of Mahomet or of the Grand Lama; and for this plain reason, that the case assumes we are a Christian people, and the morality of the country is deeply ingrafted upon Christianity, and not upon the doctrines or worship of those imposters.[3]

In other words, the thought that state constitutions called for equal treatment of diverse religions was dismissed as outlandish. Power and respect were owed to the Christian religion, not to "imposters." This thought was repeatedly affirmed in the highest places in case any might doubt it. The U.S. Supreme Court echoed it more than once as an unquestioned matter of fact. It observed in 1844, speaking of Christianity, that its "divine origin and trust are admitted, and therefore it is not to be maliciously and openly reviled and blasphemed against."[4] Sustaining federal prosecutions of Mormons for polygamy, the Court said that practice was "contrary to the spirit of Christianity and of the civilization which Christianity has produced in the Western World.[5] In 1892 the Court saw fit to affirm expressly that "this is a Christian nation"[6] and as late as 1931, with the first Jewish Justice, Louis D. Brandeis, on the bench, it said, "We are a Christian nation."[7] The Court, in any event, has not repeated that kind of utterance since 1931, and Justice Brennan recently condemned these expressions as "arrogant."[8]

As for blasphemy, no longer known to American law, it was the subject of an intriguing English case decided in 1990. Salman Rushdie, in addition to wide critical acclaim for his novel *The Satanic Verses*, drew the less welcome consequence of being targeted by Iran's theocratic ruler, the Ayatollah Khomeini, who issued a fatwa (a species of religious edict) in February 1989 calling upon loyal Muslims to murder him and his publishers for insulting Islam. Forced into hiding, Rushdie probably found it much less alarming as a relative matter when a Muslim applicant sought under English procedure to have him prosecuted for blasphemy. A high English court upheld a magistrate who refused to start the prosecution, ruling that the proposed charge of blasphemy could not validly be brought under the law of England.[9] So far, so good.

The reason for the decision is less delightful. English law, the court held, does not include any notion of blasphemy against the religion of Islam, or, indeed, against any religion other than Christianity. In other words, the crime of blasphemy is still extant in Britain to punish robust attacks on Christianity alone, or, as the court also appeared to say, on the Church of England alone, excluding other Protestant, and certainly Catholic, denominations.

If that sounds to you like a slightly creepy anomaly, it does to me as well. It may on analysis be somewhat less grisly than the bare summary suggests. Having no written constitution, and plainly no judicial review of statutes, Britain has a parliament that is supreme. That is, a law on the books cannot be invalidated by the courts. The law of blasphemy, going way back, has never been repealed, and the courts evidently are powerless to enlarge or contract or erase it. So the decision keeping blasphemy narrow, and apparently little used, if used at all, is less repulsive than it might at first seem. We are entitled still to find it repulsive enough and to congratulate ourselves on having no comparable anachronism to contend with.

Reverting to our own history, I've noted that through much of the nineteenth century, and into the twentieth, the prevailing notion was that this was "a Christian nation," meaning a Protestant nation. The bitter animus against Roman Catholics that had marked the colonial era did not end with the adoption of the Articles of Federation or the writing of the Constitution in 1787. Despite their close counterparts of the First Amendment, a number of states continued, with the acquiescence of the judges, to enforce or countenance discrimination against Catholics.

Catholics in the 1840s fought against the reading of the King James Bible in the public schools; the disagreement took the form of physical violence in Philadelphia, the City of Brotherly Love. A Massachusetts court held it permissible for a public-school teacher to beat a Catholic pupil for refusing to read aloud the Protestant version of the Ten Commandments.[10] A child in Maine was held properly expelled for the same offense.[11] Though governmental discrimination disappeared, the presidential election of 1928 displayed the broad and bitter vein of anti-Catholic sentiment among the forces defeating Alfred E. Smith. The animus was by no means spent when it was overcome, along with other obstacles, in the close victory of John F. Kennedy in 1960.

As is true for too many other religious groups, the Roman Catholic priesthood has exhibited a morbid tendency to adapt its views on church-state relations to the measure of its power in the secular community. The erstwhile opposition to reading from the King James Bible has become support for Bible reading in the public schools, without regard to the growing numbers for whom that is offensive—Muslims, Jews, atheists, among others. When the Supreme Court struck down an innocuous species of officially composed prayer in 1962,[12] Cardinal Spellman joined the evangelist Billy Graham, a host of other Christian leaders, and an army of devout politicians in denouncing this embrace of "the foul concept of atheism."[13]

In molding its position to its circumstances, the Catholic leadership has done no more or less than other sects over the centuries. The question, to state it bluntly, appears too often to be one of power more than principle. The sea changes of Jewish clerics from Brooklyn to Israel have been noted earlier. A couple of hundred years ago, in Virginia, James Madison denounced the Presbyterian hierarchy for a similar display of flexibility. He noted that they appeared simultaneously to oppose any established church and to desire, if it came to that, to be within the establishment:

> The Presbyterians . . . seem as ready to set up an establishment which is to take them in as they were to pull down that which shut them out. I do not know a more shameful contrast than might be found between their memorials on the latter and former occasion.[14]

This is not by any means to deny that there are deep principles at stake or to assert that no one observes them. It is to say that in matters of religion as in politics, with both domains implicating too often a quest for *power* over minds and souls as well as behavior, balances of power inevitably play a role in leadership positions. This has been and remains true everywhere. As Supreme Court Justice William O. Douglas put it: "In sectarian circles hunger for secular power is still strong the world over."[15] If that is a sadness from time to time, it is like other facts of life. It accounts for my fundamental thesis that we should so govern ourselves as to deny in the fullest possible measure the political power endlessly sought by religious groups.

The realities at all events do reflect demographic changes. And so it came to pass by the latter half of the twentieth century that while anti-Catholic sentiment among Protestant

Americans remained a palpable force, the lineups with respect to church-state relations had altered and subdivided the several faiths. In the continuing controversy over state aid to parochial schools, given their strong preference for such schools, Catholics pressed for whatever tax dollars they could capture to help foot the bills. They tended to find allies in Lutheran groups and Orthodox Jews, who also desired help in supporting their parochial schools. Large groups of Protestants, on the other hand, along with non-Orthodox Jews, fought steadily against government financial aid to sectarian schools, continuing a traditional stance that had characterized most mainstream Protestant denominations over the years. That position probably reflected in large measure the fact that until Supreme Court decisions changed this picture, the religious elements in American public schools had in fact been essentially Protestant in character.

While the issues and alliances have changed with the times, the original aspiration for a Christian America retains a significant measure of influence. The inheritors of the aspirations are no longer exclusively Protestant. Now the largest single denomination, Roman Catholics are well represented among those who insist that the religious imprint of the Christian majority should be acknowledged and proclaimed as fixing the spiritual identity of the nation as a whole. Among the many motivations for this stance is a kind of resentment that minority groups should question or resist the dominance of Christians as still the predominant group taken all together. There is sometimes an explicit, always clearly implicit, outrage that "they" (the intrusive others) are trying to deny or take over "our" patrimony.

The sentiment is not yet—one hopes it never will be— shared by anything like a majority of the Christian majority. It tends rather to be the business of very audible, very energetic minorities like fundamentalist evangelical leaders and the active groups that want crèches or crosses in public places, censorship of school and public libraries, and control of local school boards to guard against assertedly immoral and impure secular influences. The notion of a "Christian America" is by no means confined, however, to fringe elements. Fundamentalisms of various kinds appear currently to comprise a growth industry—in the United States as elsewhere around the world.

Quite apart from fundamentalism, there is a strong, persistent, and apparently earnest line of American thought holding that it is both ridiculous and painful to exclude from public and official pronouncements the recognition of Christianity as the dominant religious faith. It is one thing, this thought goes, to allow freedom for all. It is a wholly other and silly thing, given that the great majority are Christian, to exclude public and official professions of the majority faith. The concept of "toleration," this view holds, is a good and surely sufficient one for the minority beneficiaries of the essential freedom. There is no just reason to go beyond that and exclude expressions of the majority faith from public occasions.

Among the weighty proponents of this line is former Harvard Law School Dean and U.S. Solicitor General Erwin N. Griswold, fairly to be described as a liberal Protestant. In a 1963 address at the Utah Law School, Dean Griswold, as he then was, criticized the much debated decision of the Supreme Court striking down a prayer for the classroom written by the New York Board of Regents (sic).[16] The prayer, in full, was:

> Almighty God, we acknowledge our dependence upon Thee, and we beg Thy blessings upon us, our parents, our teachers and our Country.

One may be permitted to wonder how many spiritual nerves were set to tingling by that prayer. It may even be permissible to doubt the religiosity of people who need state officials to compose their prayers. Beyond any such speculations, it is a fact that the Supreme Court's decision forbidding that official prayer led to storms of protest across the country. Adding his scholarly breath to the storm, Dean Griswold recalled the Christian origins and traditions of the country. He went on to say:

> This is a country of religious toleration. That is a great consequence of our history embodied in the First Amendment. But does religious toleration mean religious sterility? I wonder why it should be thought that it does. This, I venture to say again, has been, and is, a Christian country, in origin, history, tradition and culture. It was out of Christian doctrine and ethics, I think it can be said, that it developed its notion of toleration. No one in this country can be required to have any particular form of religious belief; and no one can suffer legal discrimination because he has or does not have any particular religious belief. But does the fact that we have officially adopted toleration as our standard mean that we must give up our history and our tradition? The Moslem who comes here may worship as he pleases, and may hold public office without discrimination. That is as it should be. But why should it follow that he can require others to give up their Christian tradition merely because he is a tolerated and welcomed member of the community?[17]

We have seen from relatively high places more rough-and-tumble variants of Dean Griswold's thought that "tolerated and welcomed" people like the Muslim to whom he referred should not quibble about public recognition of the majority Christian faith. A Roman Catholic federal district judge, Frank McGarr, found his patience overextended when the American Jewish Congress objected to the emplacement of a crèche at Chicago's City Hall. Dismissing the protest, he wrote:

> These are word games we are playing. As words may, they sometimes illuminate the truth, sometimes obfuscate

it. The truth is that America's origins are Christian with the result that some of our fondest traditions are Christian, and that our founding fathers intended and achieved full religious freedom for all within the context of a Christian nation in the first amendment as it was adopted rather than as we have rewritten it.[18]

That judge was held to have broken the rules of the "word games" he was supposed to play, and his decision was duly reversed.[19] "Reversed" does not mean "disappeared." The quoted decision remains an interesting fact of life in at least a couple of respects. For one, it represents a measurable minority of judicial opinion that continues to keep alive and kicking the dissent from prevailing law separating church and state.

Second, the sentiments of Judge McGarr are a piquant reminder of how abbreviated the sense of history is in America, not least among judges. Judge McGarr, dismissing the wall of separation as a matter of "word games," happens to have been a Roman Catholic. To be sure, American judges are not identified professionally with any religious faith. But to the extent they remain human, they presumably stay aware of what they are—male, female, black, skinny, Catholic, etc. In that light, it is fairly to be noted that a Roman Catholic judge should have invoked "America's origins" in dismissing a minority religious protest as "word games." He had evidently forgotten, if he had once known, how at the time of the founding fathers Roman Catholics were variously disfavored and disqualified for being Roman Catholics. Likewise, he was presumably ignorant of the times, well after the founding fathers' era, when Roman Catholic schoolchildren were beaten and otherwise abused for insisting that things deeper than word games were at stake in their refusal to read in their own plain English language from the King James Bible.

More is involved than whether Judge McGarr's opinion

earns a flunking grade in history, as it surely does. The fundamental *legal* error, worse for a judge than failing in history, is the neglect of what minority rights mean in our constitutional order. One supposes that even this judge who saw fit to refer to our "Christian nation" would have known better by 1986 than to speak of our "*white* nation." Yet we are, by head count, leaving aside the slovenly description of skin color, nearly as much a white as a Christian nation. Nobody civilized would so describe us, however, because it is incorrect and outrageous in any sense that counts.

The arrogant error of labeling us a "Christian nation" is not better. Nor is it beautified, as some have thought, by calling us "Judeo-Christian." If anything, it is deepened. This, again, is not a matter of numbers; if it were, "Islamo-Christian" would soon work better when American Muslims outnumber American Jews and continue gaining rapidly on Christians. Apart from numbers, the hyphenated adjective is used only to trivialize differences and to obliterate history by a phony homogenization. The hyphen is scarcely large enough to conceal, and should cause no one to overlook, that more Jews than are now alive have been killed by Christians for the sin of being Jews. Whether one shares either faith, it is stupid as well as disrespectful to forget how many hundreds of millions of people have thought the differences between them marked the separation between supreme truth and damnable falsity. This is not to doubt that the regime of deadly enmity should have given way long ago to a widened effort by Jews and Christians to forgive and even to love one another. It is only to say that the route to that consummation is not charted by labels that serve as camouflage.

The broader point remains that no label, however embracive it might sound, fairly describes the "religion" of America because there is by constitutional definition no American religion. For every public and legal purpose that matters, we are neither religious nor irreligious—not adherents or opponents of any religion of any kind. Underscore "public" and "legal." This is, vitally, a question of public law. By the very same token—by virtue of the same constitutional principles—we are all free, one at a time and in nongovernmental groups as large as we can muster, to join in religious faiths as devotedly as we please. That is, of course, the essential assurance of the Free Exercise Clause. There is no conflict between that and the Establishment Clause, as some have thought, but an entire harmony and mutual reinforcement. The two leave us each free to believe as we are led to believe, with none of us coerced by the power of the state. In this setting, the notion of "disbelief" falls away as a matter of public interest since it refers almost always only to someone's failure to share someone else's beliefs.

The sound perception of today's Supreme Court—that neither religion nor nonreligion is the province of government—has been missed equally by Justices otherwise far apart on the ideological spectrum. It was no part of either judicial wisdom or sound legal doctrine for Justice Douglas to declaim for the Court in 1952 that "we are a religious people whose institutions presuppose a Supreme Being." If most of us are religious, many of us are not, and today's majority no more makes us all a religious people than another day's different majority might make us an irreligious or nonreligious people.

A comparable conclusion applies to the expressions forty years later of Justice Scalia when he decried the majority's decision against a publicly sponsored graduation prayer that he found "inspiring" while others, no less entitled to respect for their preferences under the First Amendment, evidently found it objectionable, if not merely banal. Commissioned to enforce the Constitution neutrally, without regard to personal religious preference, the Justice found it appropriate to advise lawyers and others on how to trivialize or nullify the Court's decision so that "graduates and their parents may proceed to thank God, as Americans have always done, for the blessings

He has generously bestowed on them and their country.[20] The fact is, of course, that not all Americans, while remaining Americans, no less than others, have thanked God in Scalia's or the majority's fashion. The rights of sundry minorities are blandly neglected in the Justice's insistence on official promotion of public prayers premised on his conviction that "religious believers" are led to feel affection for each other by "voluntarily joining in prayer together, to the God whom they all worship and seek."[21] The volumes of Supreme Court reports are no more adorned by such sentiments than they would be if some future atheist on the Court chose similarly to propound her different views on ultimate things.

Politicians and other people who should know better regularly link the picture of Americans as a "religious people" with the proposition that democracy has its origins in the principles of Judaism and Christianity. Like other certainties that go without saying, this is said very often. It also resembles such certainties in being false. Familiar history records that the initially theocratic Hebrews and then the otherworldly Christians, from their beginnings and for many centuries thereafter, did not in fact create or cause democratic forms of government. On the contrary, both lived comfortably with, and themselves exemplified, authoritarian regimes. Wherever one looks (at least outside non-Judeo-Christian ancient Greece) in all the centuries before the eighteenth—say, at the Crusades, the Inquisition, feudalism, American slavery, the divinely righteous kings—the picture is anything but democratic. To be sure, ethical principles taught by the great religions are cherished in the democratic ethos. The fact remains that ideas like caring for your neighbor and respecting individual worth are ancient (and steadily ignored) while democracy is brand-new.

The absence of the tie between religion and democracy is striking in relatively modern as well as ancient times. Long after the Enlightenment philosophers led the way in the United

States and France, borrowing more from ancient Greece and Rome than from the Bible, the churches continued to subsist comfortably with repressive governments. The fascist governments of the Latin countries in both hemispheres, perhaps most notably the Spanish Church and Franco, are only the most dramatic cases. David Hume may have overstated the case when he wrote that "in all ages of the world priests have been enemies to liberty."[22] That indictment was excessive and one-sided and is even more so today. It remains not merely excessive but plainly mistaken to credit the churches with having authored or inspired the ideas of democracy and democratic freedoms.

For all the great religious leaders and for all the undoubted virtues of their followers, there is no evidence that adherents of the dominant faiths, taken all together, are any more democratic, more moral, or better citizens than people of other faiths or of no religion. The springs of moral excellence are more mysterious and complex than we so far know. However the prized qualities are derived, it is not the case, nor should it be, that people are good because God leads them to be. "The moral monster who thinks there is nothing morally wrong in torturing a child except that God has forbidden it, has a parallel in the moralist who will not treat the fact that the child will suffer agony as in itself a moral reason enough."[23] The point was put by Plato much longer ago in the *Euthyphro*, where Socrates opined that the good is not good because of the gods' approval but rather is approved by the gods because it is good.

There are in sum ancient and modern grounds for seeking the good secular government in earthly secular arrangements. When I speak of a "secular government" in this setting, the focus is upon a government that neither seeks to control nor is controlled by any religious group or doctrine. And the word "religious" for this purpose covers the wide spectrum from the dominant sects to beliefs of every species about the ultimate things addressed by religion. It includes, for instance, the concepts of "aggressive atheism" perceived by John Dewey "to have something in common with traditional supernaturalism."[24] The wall of separation would insulate government from Soviet-style thought control involving those concepts no less than the kind we think of more customarily as religious. The present mix of religious adherents in America is not more likely to be permanent than other human arrangements. That may well be true of the Supreme Court's wisdom in demanding (usually) that government maintain a strictly detached neutrality with respect to all religion and nonreligion. The best finite hope for the long time being is that we can preserve this precious safeguard for the peace and spiritual liberty of all of us.

4

PIETY VERSUS

"SECULAR HUMANISM":

A PHONY WAR

THE decision of the Supreme Court in 1962 outlawing the bland triviality composed as a prayer by the New York Board of Regents,[1] and then the succeeding year's ruling against Bible reading in the public schools,[2] led to a thunder of opposition that keeps rolling and resounding over the years. There was outrage that God had been "expelled" from the public schools. A senator declared that the Supreme Court had "made God unconstitutional." Proposed constitutional amendments to overturn those decisions became staple contributions to the congressional hopper. A measure supporting public-school prayers became a central plank of the Republican platform, endorsed by President Reagan with the kind of folksy passion that lifted his high popularity ratings. While that position has never commanded the two-thirds vote in Congress required to launch an amendment, it appears steadily to enlist a large majority in American public opinion polls. It is reflected, too, in a wide and persistent defiance of the Supreme Court's ruling as local communities, especially in the South, cheer schoolteachers for their classroom prayers, promote prayers on athletic fields, and continue to act as if officially directed sanctimony might be a path to salvation.

A strong band of pious politicians have campaigned during the last third of the twentieth century for the right of students, as it is said, to engage in voluntary, silent prayer in the public schools. A number of states in the 1980s enacted statutes to implement this goal. To avoid the constitutional rule against open and explicit group prayers in the schools, legislators combined religious zeal with legal genius. A more or less standard law simply ordered a "moment of silence" during the school day, when every student individually could think about nothing, solve mathematical puzzles, fantasize about sex, or even—perhaps—pray. In a number of instances the state law said nothing at all about prayer, providing only for the brief period of silence. These paths for God's re-entry into the public schools have for the most part run into judicial roadblocks, though the cases have not been unanimous and the struggle is not yet over.

Virginia's silent-prayer law reached, and expired in, the Supreme Court in 1985.[3] The statute struck down in that case provided for a period of silence in the public schools "for meditation or voluntary prayer." Ishmael Jaffree, father of two second-graders and one kindergartner, sued to have that enactment invalidated. Sustaining his position (over the dissents of Chief Justice Warren Burger and Justices Byron White and William Rehnquist), the Supreme Court found that the purpose of passing the law was, as an Alabama senator put it,[4] "to return voluntary prayer to our public schools." That violated the state's duty of neutrality with respect to religion under the Establishment Clause.

However, two of the Justices in the majority said, and four

broadly intimated, that a law merely providing for a period of silence would pass constitutional muster. And that echoed a long-running debate that remains at most only partially resolved. The idea of legislatively decreed moments of silence in the public schools has appealed to the lawmakers of more than half the states. It has led to a spate of judicial opinions one way or another and a small shelf of scholarly writing. For all the devout attention they have received, these state laws exhibit only two or three salient—and to me regrettable—characteristics.

First, they all emerge in the wake of the Supreme Court's banning of officially sponsored prayer and Bible reading in the schools. Their background leaves no question about their essential purpose, to evade or fight in the rearguard against that ban.

Second, in a number of cases the sponsors of these acts make no bones about their view that the majority has taken more than an acceptable amount of guff from minorities, and that the preponderant sentiment favoring school prayer should have its way. A New Jersey state assemblyman sponsoring one of the bills was asked in debate about its effect on atheists. The question may have wrongly implied that only atheists would oppose this sort of law. The answer in its way dismissed all sorts of opponents when the assemblyman said that "they were so few in number their views could be discounted."[5] That position is by no means rare. In an opinion upholding the Nebraska legislature's regular payment and use of a Presbyterian minister to open its sessions with a prayer, Chief Justice Burger wrote that this was "simply a tolerable acknowledgement of beliefs widely held among the people of this country."[6] Expressions like these, made in upholding religious exercises under government sponsorship, give less than enthusiastic support to the proposition that the Religion Clauses vouchsafe minority rights, not indulgences for the majority.

A third characteristic of the moment-of-silence laws is a common claim of their sponsors: that they are merely neutral provisions for a time of repose in the school day, when students can do as they please, even pray if the spirit moves them. This has august support, in the Supreme Court and among notable legal scholars. I'll explain below my dissent from this position.

At this point, to conclude on the state of the law as of now, I report that the majority of the lower federal courts that have considered the question have held these moment-of-silence statutes unconstitutional. They have perceived usually a more or less veiled purpose to sponsor or to promote prayer. One noteworthy case led a federal district judge to strike down under the federal Constitution a West Virginia constitutional amendment, no less, by which West Virginia statesmen had undertaken to sidestep the Supreme Court's rulings.[7] The West Virginia Amendment said:

> Public schools shall provide a designated brief time at the beginning of each school day for any student desiring to exercise their right to personal and private contemplation, meditation, or prayer. No student of a public school may be denied their right to personal and private contemplation, meditation or prayer nor shall any student be required or encouraged to engage in any given contemplation, meditation or prayer as a part of the school curriculum.

There were worse things wrong with that amendment than the ungainly use of "their" as a singular pronoun. In the course of his opinion, the federal judge quoted the words of an "eleven-year-old child of the Jewish faith [who] testified as follows" concerning his early experience in school under the amendment:

A. Well, then the next day our principal read the whole sheet of guidelines [under the amendment for meditation or prayer] to us. Then we had the moment of silence and I read a book during it.

Q. Okay. Did, what kind of book did you read?

A. Science fiction.

Q. Okay. A fantasy book?

A. Uh-huh.

Q. Do you understand the difference between fantasy and reality?

A. Uh-huh.

Q. Do you like fantasy books?

A. Yep.

Q. Okay. Did anything happen or did anybody say anything to you during home room about that?

A. No.

Q. Okay. How long did the, did the period last?

A. I'm not exactly sure. It may have been a minute, may have been thirty seconds. I don't know.

Q. You say that they read something to you. You referred to the guidelines. Do you remember the substance of any of those, what they did?

A. Well, basically they said, they told us how long it was supposed to be and quite a few times they kept saying, "contemplation, meditation, and prayer," and then towards the end they told us that if we had any religious questions, we would be referred to our parents or to, I think the phrase was "a leader of our faith," but I am not exactly sure about the phrasing.

Q. And then after that what was said?

A. After that, we did the Pledge of Allegiance.

Q. Okay. Did you participate in the Pledge of Allegiance?

A. Yes.

Q. Okay. And were there announcements?

A. I don't think there were very many that day.

Q. Okay. And then what happened after the bell rang?

A. Well, we all went to first period.

Q. Okay. Anything happen to you in first period?

A. No.

Q. Okay. How about second period?

A. Well, in second period, which was science, our teacher left the room to go find something and one of the people who was in my home room turned around and asked me why I had been reading a book during the moment of silence. And I told him that I didn't have to pray then and I didn't want to and then he told me that I should be praying all the time and then he said something to the effect that if I prayed all the time, maybe I could go to heaven with all the Christians when Jesus came for the second time instead of, as he put it, going down with all the other Jews.

Q. Okay. Are you a member of the Jewish faith?

A. Uh-huh.

Q. That's your religion?

A. Uh-huh.

Q. Did he know that you were a member of that faith?

A. Yes, he did.

Q. Okay. And do you know what he meant about going to heaven or going down?

A. Well, I think he, from what—

Q. What did it mean to you?

A. Well, I think it meant that he was saying that certain people were going to all go to heaven. I mean, it didn't make much sense to me because I don't know anything about his faith and that the rest of the people were going to, you know, be stuck someplace if they didn't believe in the right things.

Q. Okay. Did he say what the right things were to believe in?

A. Uh-huh.

Q. What did he say?

A. Well, he said that you should believe in Christ basically.

Q. Okay. Did you say anything to him?

A. I tried to explain to him that I had my own beliefs and that I went by, I followed my beliefs and not his and, you know, when the time came, it was going to be my problem and not his.

Q. Did anybody else participate in the conversation?

A. Yes. There was another person who, this first boy told another boy that the Jews only used the Old Testament and they didn't use the New Testament and this other boy thought that it was really stupid and then there was some period of another, of more speech, more conversation that I don't remember, but then the second boy said something to the effect that, why was he even trying to talk to me because the Jews weren't worth saving because they had killed Christ and that was about the end of it.

Q. Okay. Did you say anything after that or—

A. Well, I, not really, I just, I guess I said, I just told him it was my right not to pray and he, I had my rights and he had his.

Q. Okay. How did you feel about that?

A. Well, I felt, you know, hurt. Then I kind of felt angry because I didn't think it was fair that he should be able to say things like that during school and get away with it. I also felt kind of uncomfortable because it's kind of hard to try and tell somebody that, who keeps on talking that you are not listening to them.

Q. Okay. Did you, did you talk with your teacher?

A. No, I didn't.

Q. Any reason that you didn't or—

A. Well, I was afraid that the teacher either wouldn't listen or if the teacher did listen, there would be a big issue made out of it and I would be in the limelight for the wrong reasons and I was afraid that I could have a lot of bad publicity, I guess you'd say, from that.

Q. Okay. You mean in your school?

A. Uh-huh.[8]

The opinion went on to summarize other interesting aspects of the testimony, including these:

A Baptist pastor testified that he objects to prayer "in a school setting where everyone else is praying as an act of religious faith and so forth, not because one could do that just because everyone else is doing it, it's something one chooses or affirms for himself or herself."

The pastor said, "It tends to trivialize one's religious devotion and that makes it, well, it sometimes borders on sacrilege."

A 12-year-old boy of the Roman Catholic faith testified he is afraid to challenge his teacher's directions to stand and pray each morning because he might receive demerits for "doing wrong or disobeying the teacher." Other witnesses representing the Lutheran, Roman Catholic, Moslem and Jewish faiths and the teaching and psychology professions also testified in opposition to the Amendment.

In addition to the quoted evidence, the judge had before him a record that gave evidence of a state legislature bent on advising the Supreme Court of its errors. One state senator explained: "To me separation of church and state concept is a myth, like evolution." A house delegate said: "I believe it is time when we should welcome God back into the classrooms and not by just meditation but by prayer and praise also." Similarly devout sentiments were echoed by other West Virginia legislators standing in a large and courageous majority on the side of God.

With the kind of evidence before him, the judge said the question was a "relatively simple one" under the precedents, and that it was his duty to strike down the West Virginia amendment. Before performing that duty, however, the judge found himself moved to tell how strained he found the quality of justice in this case:[9]

From a personal and moral standpoint, however, the decision herein contained is the most difficult one with which this Court has ever been faced and indeed, is likely as exacting as any which will ever come before it.

The judge found it necessary to say that even though he said elsewhere that he could not

> refrain from observing that in [his] opinion a hoax conceived in political expediency has been perpetrated upon those sincere citizens of West Virginia who voted for this amendment to the West Virginia Constitution in the belief that even if it violated the United States Constitution, "majority rule" would prevail. There is no such provision in the Constitution.

He later explained the possible inconsistency when he observed that he

> anticipates continuing adverse reaction to [his] decision but considers [his] obligation to uphold the United States Constitution to be a duty which cannot in good conscience be shirked because of intimidation.[10]

Sentiments like that may not be in the most elegantly stoical style of the best federal judges. They reflect, though, the relentless pressures that should leave no one smug about the security of the safeguards for minority consciences in America.

Credit the West Virginia federal judge, in any event, with enforcing the law against the blunt defiance of the West Virginia legislature. Other legislators have chosen to be more subtle and to insist that their decreed periods of silence really have nothing to do with the Constitution's prohibition against officially promoted prayer in the public schools. And, as I've said, august judges and scholars have accepted this account. A law professor who vigorously supports a liberally interpreted Establishment Clause has written that laws decreeing moments of silence are no problem if they do not prescribe prayer during those moments; the students, he points out, have free choice: some "may use the moment of silence to pray; others may use it to meditate, daydream, plot mischief, or ogle their favorite classmate."[11] Justices of the Supreme Court and other federal judges have reached the same conclusion.[12] With all respect to them, I'm led to recall the observation of Justice Oliver Wendell Holmes that judges tend to be naïve people. Granted that he probably had, as usual, a more layered meaning than the one I now take, it does seem remarkably naïve to treat the moment-of-silence laws in this innocent fashion.

To be sure, the decreed time of silence may be used to daydream or ogle, etc. But how did it happen that in all the decades before the school-prayer cases no powerhouse of daydreamers and oglers (who represent all of us, after all) demanded laws compelling stated periods of silence? Rhetorical questions don't need answers. As a relevant tangent, however, one recalls the long stretches of silence, in study halls and classrooms, that characterized life in public school. There was always plenty of time to pray or ogle. No law proclaimed a specific moment of silence. No occasion arose when anybody was questioned about the failure to use the silent time for praying. The moment-of-silence laws are, in one word, charades.

Ruses of this kind remind us of the essentially sleazy uses to which politicians put their professed devotion to God. The Christians among them notably forget the lesson Christ taught about this:

> Beware of practicing your piety before men in order to be seen by them; for then you will have no reward from your Father who is in heaven.[13]

Instead, in a kind of guerrilla war against the First Amendment, periodic bursts of public religious displays by government officials are offered up as substitutes for statesmanship. A further example or two may be enough illustration.

During the Civil War, when the fate of the nation seemed precarious, the Union cause was buttressed in 1864 by the placement of the national motto, "In God We Trust," on a two-cent piece. Blessed by the Congress, that sentiment on the money continued unquestioned until it came to be noticed by President Theodore Roosevelt. It struck him as being "close to sacrilege." He noted that this form of affirmation had tended to produce jokes rather than accesses of elevated faith. In a letter to a clergyman he wrote:

> Every one must remember the innumerable cartoons and articles based on phrases like "In God we trust for the other eight cents"; "In God we trust for the short weight"; "In God we trust for the thirty-seven cents we do not pay"; and so forth, and so forth.[14]

More repelled than amused, Roosevelt ordered that the motto be deleted from the currency.

One man's sacrilege is a lot of other people's holiness. The Congress was appalled by the President's vandalism and ordered the slogan put back onto the money. Both our metal and paper forms of legal tender have been graced ever since by the religious motto.

Do you feel better protected by those words on the money? Does it perhaps help to keep the dollar sound? Do you in fact have any awareness that the words are there? Probably the answer for most of us is that by this time it is a matter of little or no consequence. If it was thought about, however, one might hope, though possibly in vain, that more of us would be ready to join in Theodore Roosevelt's sentiments. For the genuinely devout, the vote of confidence in God, on money, of all places, might fairly seem an affront. For the nonreligious or for those, like Buddhists, among others, to whom the trust in God is an alien concept, the routine affirmation by their government might grate. It is difficult to know in the end how in a country never accused of insufficiently worshipping money anyone finds strength or solace in this practice. At least in my judgment, all of us, and the still generally shared concept of God, are diminished a little by such cheap public expressions of religiosity.

The thought was put more felicitously by a sensitive Harvard law teacher in a lovely book attending devotedly to the springs of religious sentiment as well as to the sound place of democratic government. Speaking of the easy manifestations of official spirituality, he counted these as instances of "chauvinism and religiosity" combining "to produce a triumphant vulgarity" that congratulates God for the wisdom of favoring America and Americans over lesser, less godly nations.[15]

Vulgarity is not necessarily unconstitutionality. One earnest separationist sued some years ago to have the national motto and its display on the currency declared unconstitutional. Rejecting his claim, a federal appeals court said:

> It is quite obvious that the national motto and the slogan on coinage and currency "In God We Trust" has nothing whatsoever to do with the establishment of religion. Its use is of a patriotic or ceremonial character and bears no true resemblance to a governmental sponsorship of a religious exercise.[16]

In its cool legal fashion, that characterization reminds us that there are governmental things worse than constitutional infractions. Wherever one stands with respect to belief in God, it can hardly give comfort or satisfaction to have the Deity subjected to empty, nonreligious uses "of a patriotic or ceremonial character." The bland amalgamation of God and the state, while it may meet the test of the Establishment Clause, leads at best to a kind of cant that all of us may find embarrassing.

In the same class, though perhaps more debatably, I'd put the improvement on the Pledge of Allegiance fashioned by Congress in 1954. That was a year, it will be recalled, when Senator Joseph McCarthy was still exploring how low we might be sunk in his ersatz but grimly destructive crusade against "subversives." It was also a year McCarthy's colleagues found it meet to insert the words "under God" after the reference to this "one nation" in the pledge. The House Report on the bill that became this law said that "it would serve to deny the atheistic and materialistic concepts of communism with its attendant subservience of the individual."[17] Some very brief remarks on the floor reaffirmed that inserting the words "under God" would "strengthen the national resistance to communism."[18] The only cerebration manifested on the subject of the bill had to do with the number and placement of commas in the revised pledge—i.e., whether it should be simply "one nation under God" or "one Nation, under God," as the legislative judgment finally determined. The short debate on this subject was suitably placid. There was no debate at all on the merits of the revision and no vote against it. Who, after all, would be caught in the open excluding God?

The uses of God as a "ceremonial and patriotic" implement go forward steadily in more obtrusive and questionable forms. The insistent demand to have crèches and menorahs in public sites continues to present tough questions leading to the varieties of intricate and disputed answers mentioned in Chapter 1. The legal issues are tricky enough to promise a continued supply of test cases. To oversimplify a lot, the hardest cases —where private groups want to put their crèches or menorahs in the public park or on City Hall plaza—pit the First Amendment free-speech rights of those groups against the claim of the objectors that this placement of the symbols indicates government endorsement of the religion symbolized. Without questioning the difficulty of these cases, it is fair to conjure with the question why they keep happening. The answer lies, I think, in the very nature of hostile and competitive patriotism out of which one might wish that God could have been kept. The crèche on the public square—to "put Christ back into Christmas," as its sponsors regularly say—plants the religious flag of the angry nativists winning theirs back from the alien, infidel intruders. (Who do they think they are?) The menorah sponsors are a kindred but more pathetic story. (If the *goyim* can do it, so can we.) Both are joined together as enemies of the mutual forbearance that is at the heart of religious freedom in a pluralist society.

The gist of the demand is that the muscle of your religion be displayed in the public space. The subject, as is usual with facile shows of patriotism, is power. It is put, to be sure, as a matter of free expression by the crèche and menorah advocates, but that is largely fraud or self-delusion. There are ample private spaces in every community, amply visible, for displaying religious icons. The insistence on the *public* space, the space that belongs to all of us, is to show those others, the nonadherents. The distinction is readily, if not always malevolently, blurred. Leonid Feldman, an earnest cleric, raised as an atheist and abused as a Jew in the former Soviet Union, serves now as a conservative rabbi in Florida. He says he is now "frightened by secularism" and perplexed by those, Jews and others, who oppose the installation of menorahs. He states his case in a few moving words: "I fought the KGB for the right to light a menorah. Forgive me if I don't want to eliminate menorahs from America's lawns."[19] Moving his words may be. They also reflect, in brief compass, an entire confusion about what church-state separation means in the United States.

The fear of "secularism" is a chimera. "Secular" is what our government is supposed to be. That has nothing to do with the *imposed* religion of atheism that Rabbi Feldman suffered in the U.S.S.R. As for the right to light menorahs on "America's lawns," the rabbi should surely have realized by now that it is a right fully respected under our law (leaving aside blights like private anti-Semitism and other "antis" that continue to sully religious, racial, and ethnic relationships in our country and most others).

Whatever misunderstandings may beset a recent refugee from Soviet atheism, there is no ground for similar confusion, and probably no similar confusion, among most people who want their religious symbols standing on public property. The symbols make a statement—not of religious faith. They are not needed for that. They assert simply and starkly, as I've said, power over the nonbelievers. This was underscored for me in a fleeting moment of a case that ended 4–4 in the Supreme Court, the equal division (Justice Powell was ill and absent) resulting in a defeat for the village of Scarsdale (with me as unsuccessful counsel) when it sought to deny a place for a crèche in a public circle.[20] In the course of that proceeding, one of the sponsors of the crèche was asked about his interest in viewing it while it stood on Scarsdale's Boniface Circle during the Christmas season. To my surprise as the questioner, it turned out that he never bothered to go look at the crèche at all, let alone to admire or draw inspiration from it. But on reflection that should not have been so surprising. The crèche was not there for him to see or appreciate for its intrinsic spiritual value in his religious universe. It was there for others, who professed other religions or none, so that the clout of his religious group should be made manifest—above all to any in the sharply divided village who would have preferred that it not be there. This is the low road followed by at least a good number of those who seek for their religion and its symbols the imprimatur of government. If it is religious at all, this stance betokens a weak and self-doubting species of faith.

Much more blatant and unsettling than the crèches and menorahs, and even the tasteless evasions of moment-of-silence laws, is the ongoing course of flat-out defiance of the Supreme Court's ban against organized prayer in the public schools. It is ironic at best that in God's name, while tracing the blessings of democracy to their religion, so many people hack at the most vital of democratic organs: the rule of law, including the acceptance of authoritative decisions by those commissioned to expound the Constitution. Ironic or not, the practice continues, at a steep price in human anguish and political subversion. One more example helps to sharpen the picture.

In 1993, the Federal Court of Appeals embracing Texas heard the case of a junior-high-school basketball coach who regularly led his girls' team in a recitation of the Lord's Prayer at the beginning and end of each practice session.[21] At games against other schools, the members of the team were brought to the center of the court, where they got on their hands and knees while the coach stood over them, and with their heads bowed, recited the Lord's Prayer. The prayer was also said before they left school for games away from home and at critical times in games like last-second buzzer-beater shots. A twelve-year-old team member objected to the prayer. When her father spoke to the assistant superintendent of schools about her objection, that official said that "unless [the father] had grandparents buried in the Duncanville Cemetery, he had no right to tell [the assistant superintendent] how to run his schools." When Jane Doe decided not to participate in the team prayers, the coach had her stand aside at games while the others prayed. Her fellow students asked, "Aren't you a Christian?" One spectator stood up after a game and yelled, "Well, why isn't she praying? Isn't she a Christian?" Her history teacher called her "a little atheist" during one class lecture.

The court upheld an injunction forbidding this practice. No one can doubt the correctness of the decision. What causes doubt and worry is that the coach and the superintendent should have found it justifiable to require that such a lawsuit be brought. If they have done useful service at all, it is to remind us of the misery inflicted by self-righteous tyrants like these on young people and others who do not share their religious convictions (assuming in their favor that people of this sort have genuine inner "convictions" rather than merely devices for oppressing their neighbors). It is doubtful that the coach, serving as backup minister, thought this performance made his team play more effectively.

But who knows? The uses to which athletes and others put their God are multifarious and often surprising. I recall, having made a note of it, the night of October 25, 1986, when the New York Mets won the critical sixth game of the World Series on a dubious fielding effort by the Boston Red Sox first baseman. As a proper Mets fan, I stayed with the telecast to hear some post-game wisdom. Two of the star Mets players gave similar explanations for their victory. Third baseman Ray Knight explained that the Good Lord had been on their side. Catcher Gary Carter attributed the victory to the favor shown the Mets by Jesus Christ. Even a Mets fan was led to wonder how the Deity had come to nurse hostility toward the Red Sox.

Seemingly more spacious and high-minded are the clerics and philosophers who do not invoke a necessarily partisan God but argue earnestly that the secularization of government in our time leaves a moral vacuum that will be filled with false, evil, probably fascistic substitutes for true religion. A lively proponent of this position is Roman Catholic Father Richard John Neuhaus, whose famous book, *The Naked Public Square: Religion and Democracy in America*, was published in 1984, when he was a Lutheran minister. When the public square becomes naked, he taught, of religious affirmations and frankly religious morality, we lose the most basic need of a good society, some "final inhibition of evil."[22] That inhibition, he makes clear, is found in the Christian—he sometimes says "Judeo-Christian"—tradition. He faults the Supreme Court for straying in recent years from its earlier sound perception, for it remains correct in his view to acknowledge that "this is, as the Supreme Court said in 1931, a Christian people."[23] While the majority of the Court and most legal scholars rejoice that the Court would shun a repetition of that arrogant thought (as Justice Brennan called it), Father Neuhaus deems this a tragic retreat. This epitomizes, in my opinion, the profound error of his way.

As I argued earlier, it is plain wrong to aver that the fundamental morality of our strikingly diverse people is tied to Christian, or even Judeo-Christian, doctrine or observance. Throughout American history, the great politico-moral issues that have troubled and divided us have seen the Christian and Jewish clergy about as divided as everyone else. Abortion in our time, capital punishment, equal rights for women, even capitalism versus socialism have all had religious leaders on both sides. The most tragic of our national sins, slavery, saw a similar division, with the majority of ministers siding, as is usual, with the status quo throughout the centuries before emancipation. At least one thoughtful religious scholar finds the belief in an inerrant Bible, including its literal approval of slavery, a still significant strand of fundamentalist thought in the American South.[24] None of this is to doubt for an instant the value of spiritual leaders for their followers. It is only to stress again that this is a value that should be neither enforced nor endorsed by the state.

The notion that government must somehow be religious because most of our people are religious is a gross error. The astute observer Tocqueville concluded in the 1830s that it was precisely the separation of church and state that led to both the peaceful careers of varying sects and the flourishing of religion in general.[25] Times have undoubtedly changed since then, but he found among both priests and laypeople a unanimity of opinion on this score. That opinion was sound in Tocqueville's day. We should cherish and preserve it.

5

ADJUSTING CAESAR'S
LAWS TO GOD'S

When the authors of the First Amendment enjoined Congress (ultimately any organ of government at any level) from prohibiting the free exercise of religion, they set the scene for a long train of exquisitely difficult questions. Suppose your religion calls for ceremonial wine in a dry state. Or mind-altering drugs, forbidden by the narcotics laws. What if you believe sincerely that God has ordained polygamy and that the failure to take more than one wife is punishable by eternal damnation? If your religion calls for human sacrifice, no one will doubt that the state has the power to stop or punish you. On the other side, do you doubt that a way will be found in a dry state—was found during Prohibition—to make an exception from the ban against alcoholic beverages? If that is so, what about the Native American Indian Church's preference for peyote over alcohol, where both are forbidden but neither wins out clearly as the more destructive?

These questions, as lawyers will recognize, arise from some of the familiar cases under the Free Exercise Clause. The varying answers at different times mark a usually sensitive effort by the Supreme Court to define principled limits on the power of the state to limit the freedom *to act* on religious beliefs. Note the emphasis on action. Though it has not always been so, the freedom of *belief* as such, including freedom from any governmental pressure to profess beliefs one does not hold, is by now fairly securely settled. As late as 1961, Maryland's constitution had a Pickwickian provision saying there could be no test oath for public office "other than a declaration of belief in the existence of God . . ." An aspiring notary public named Torcaso earned legal immortality when he won appointment to the office but was then denied his notary's commission because he refused to declare a belief in God's existence. Maryland's highest court thought the denial of the commission was all right. A unanimous U.S. Supreme Court reversed.[1] It may reflect only the lucidity of hindsight to wonder why the Maryland Court of Appeals needed to be taught that by the Supreme Court.

The broader reminder from Torcaso's case is that, even for the freedom of belief, the right may not be, always and everywhere, absolute or absolutely clear. It took two rounds in the Supreme Court during World War II for the children of Jehovah's Witnesses to win the right, on grounds of religious conviction, to refrain from participating in the schoolroom flag salute.[2] And a stubbornly principled New Hampshire Jehovah's Witness was dragged all the way to the U.S. Supreme Court by the state of New Hampshire before he was able to vindicate his religious grounds for covering over on his automobile license plates the motto "Live Free or Die."[3] People of goodwill and democratic faith have thought the latter case to go pretty far. Whatever one's views on that, it helps to keep our liberties robust and uncramped when varieties of nonconformists probe the limits from time to time.

Apart from the few cases that test the borders of First Amendment doctrine, the freedom to believe as one pleases, and to withhold expressions of belief that are alien or offensive to one's religious convictions, seems to be solidly secured for Americans. And that is no small thing. The tiny minorities, and the deviants who look like cranks to the majority for fretting about things like the slogans on their license plates, are in the end the guardians of freedom's outposts for the rest of us. When we face facts about belief and hypocrisy, we are reminded that the chantings of piety are the easiest thing in the world for many who believe very little and very thinly. Justice Black, writing for the Court in the *Torcaso* case, re-called the observations on this subject of our third Chief Jus-tice, Oliver Ellsworth, who had been a member of the Constitutional Convention:

> In short, test-laws are utterly ineffectual: they are no se-curity at all; because men of loose principles will, by an external compliance, evade them. If they exclude any per-sons, it will be honest men, men of principle, who will rather suffer an injury, than act contrary to the dictates of their consciences . . .[4]

Ellsworth's wisdom is or should be common knowledge. It does not stop us, though it should, from regularly rewarding the hypocrites while we denounce and abuse the principled dissenters for dissenting.

For all that, in the eye of the law at least, the constitutional freedom of belief is well entrenched. Not so with *conduct* that is the product of sincere religious belief but happens to collide with legal prohibitions. Cases of this kind, ranging from po-lygamy to peyote, have tested the promises of the First Amend-ment. The Supreme Court has on the whole paid respectful attention to unpopular demands for religious freedom, prob-ably more respectful for the familiar and agreeable sects than for those that seem alien or challenging. This is another quarter in which nonjudicial officers wielding the power of government might make better use of their discretion to deflect or avoid some of the hot potatoes that wind up on the judicial plate.

The questions seemed easier, and the answers more blunt, when this subject first found a place on the Supreme Court's docket. When the Mormons were still early settlers, after having struggled across the country against the bands of arsonists and murderers who found their religion disagreeable, their doctrine included a belief in polygamy. This was not a notion that a man might find it pleasurable to have more than one wife. It was a conviction, without doubt sincerely held, that polygamous marriages were a matter of male duty, for the breach of which the punishment was eternal damnation. With Utah still a federal territory in the 1870s, George Reynolds was prosecuted in federal court for bigamy. By the time the case came to be decided by the Supreme Court, in 1879, there was no question that he had married at least twice and no question that he had done this from a genuine conviction that it was his religious duty. A unanimous Court made fairly short work of his argument that the Free Exercise Clause protected him against the prosecution and conviction.

The Court recalled with approval Jefferson's image of the wall of separation between church and state. It acknowledged, too, that the Constitution guaranteed religious freedom. But that could not help Reynolds, who was prosecuted for what he had done, not for what he believed.

> Congress was deprived of all legislative power over mere opinion, but was left free to reach actions which were in violation of social duties or subversive of good order.[5]

The Court left no doubt that bigamy violated social duties and subverted "good order."

Polygamy has always been odious among the Northern and Western Nations of Europe and, until the establishment of the Mormon Church, was almost exclusively a feature of the life of Asiatic and African people.[6]

Having made clear where it stood on the ways of Asia and Africa, and being equally clear on the power to outlaw bigamy, the Court said the only remaining question was

whether those who make polygamy a part of their religion are excepted from the operation of the statute. If they are, then those who do not make polygamy a part of their religious belief may be found guilty and punished, while those who do must be acquitted and go free. This would be introducing a new element into criminal law. Laws are made for the government of actions, and while they cannot interfere with mere religious belief and opinions, they may with practices. Suppose one believed that human sacrifices were a necessary part of religious worship, would it be seriously contended that the civil government under which he lived could not interfere to prevent a sacrifice? Or if a wife religiously believed it was her duty to burn herself upon the funeral pile of her dead husband, would it be beyond the power of the civil government to prevent her carrying her belief into practice?

So here, as a law of the organization of society under the exclusive dominion of the United States, it is provided that plural marriages shall not be allowed. Can a man excuse his practices to the contrary because of his religious belief? To permit this would be to make the professed doctrines of religious belief superior to the law of the land, and in effect to permit every citizen to become a law unto himself. Government could exist only in name under such circumstances.[7]

And so, as matters stood in 1879, the broad language of the Supreme Court seemed to allow no room at all for exempting anyone from general criminal laws on grounds of religious faith or duty. Whether religion commanded human sacrifice or bigamy or less starkly forbidden behaviors, nobody could invoke religion to "excuse his practices" because that would be "in effect to permit every citizen to become a law unto himself." The rule was simple and unequivocal.

In this as in other respects, however, the law became more complicated during the ensuing century or so, and the stated doctrine that condemned Mr. Reynolds went quite out of style. As we'll see, by the mid-twentieth century, government had to show an affirmatively powerful justification for condemning or even disadvantaging people for following religious precepts that collided with secular laws. The fact that practices might stem from Asia or Africa or other exotic places was no longer sufficient to condemn them. The concern that religious people might claim to become laws unto themselves no longer disposed of the judicial duty to weigh specific claims and balance against them the state's opposed assertions.

If a Mormon or some other religious communicant today were to press an asserted right to practice polygamy as a religious duty, the precedent against George Reynolds would supply no satisfactory answer. It would not do to brush him off with the point that his habits sounded Asian or African. Nor would it answer him sufficiently to say that human sacrifice will not be allowed even as a religious practice. It happens that the main body of the Mormon Church, by the end of the nineteenth century, altered its understanding of polygamy as a religious commandment, although small groups appear to adhere to the former doctrine. And no other religion seems to pursue the position. So the *Reynolds* precedent has not been revisited. Furthermore, though that decision seemed to have been largely or wholly eviscerated, at least until a 1990 case we reach below, one doubts that any lawyer would comfortably have counseled bigamy as a sanctioned religious practice. But this still left, and probably leaves, an uncertain range of religiously motivated conduct for which people claim, and should be permitted to enjoy, exemptions from the literal sweep of Caesar's laws. And the answer even on bigamy is not clear beyond doubt.

A half century after George Reynolds's conviction, the Supreme Court signaled that the case against religious exemptions was more complicated than it had seemed. A Jehovah's Witness was prosecuted in Massachusetts for having her nine-year-old niece (and ward), along with her aunt, selling the group's newspapers, *Watchtower* and *Consolation*, on the streets of Brockton, Massachusetts. The Court upheld her conviction, on which she had been ordered to pay "moderate fines," against the argument that this violated her religious freedom. It was not an easy brush-off, however. The Court's opinion, by Justice Rutledge, reflected concern and appreciation for the claims of parental and religious liberty. In the end, as the majority saw it, there was a public interest in child welfare that outweighed this liberty and foreclosed the claimed exemption.[8]

Justice Frank Murphy dissented. He would have demanded more "convincing proof" that the child's service in the religious enterprise, in her aunt's company, posed a real threat to the child's health or morals or general welfare. Unconvinced of that, he also noted a factor that often lurks in these contests that look to the majority like fractious and oddball demands for special treatment. He recalled that Jehovah's Witnesses had not always been treated with Christian charity by their fellow Christians or members of other religious faiths:

> Theirs is a militant and unpopular faith, pursued with a fanatical zeal. They have suffered brutal beatings; their property has been destroyed; they have been harassed at every turn by the resurrection and enforcement of little used ordinances and statutes.[9]

In law, as in wider community relationships, the conflicts stem from the stubborn desires of minorities to be different, to do their own things. This is, of course, the exact reason for the First Amendment and therefore a basic thought that ought to be present whenever a question of the rights and the limits is confronted.

The stubborn minority fared better when another question of parental authority reached the Supreme Court in 1972. This time it was an Amish parent in Wisconsin who, along with his fellow religionists, resisted the state's school law requiring compulsory attendance until age sixteen. The Supreme Court reversed convictions for violating that law.[10] Though quite irrelevant as a matter of strict constitutional law, the Court's opinion, by Chief Justice Burger, portrayed a kind of idyllic Amish community that could have been, as it has been, the subject of a tender movie. The opinion recorded the Amish willingness to have their children finish the eighth grade, but no more. After that, they believed, in unquestioned sincerity, that the worldly influences of secular education would "endanger their salvation and that of their children."[11] Their lives, as the Court recounted, were simple, rustic, pastoral, largely devoid of modern contraptions like TV, automobiles, zippers, and other essentials of their worldly neighbors. They lived, as the opinion said, "in harmony with nature and the soil, as exemplified by the simple life of the early Christian era that continued in America during much of our early life."[12] Having sounded that appealing note for the Christian majority, the opinion went on to what a cynic might have found a bit of logrolling; it described the Amish ritual of late adolescent baptism as being "not unlike the Bar Mitzvah of the Jews," a ceremony in which the new adult commits "to abide by the rules of the church community."[13] Possibly carried away a little with this, the opinion said at a later point that religion pervades the Amish "entire way of life, regulating it with the detail of the Talmudic diet."[14]

But our cynicism must not go too far. If the Amish were portrayed as especially appealing, the fact remains that Yoder's legal victory had doctrinal importance radiating beyond his religious group. Unlike the curt rejection of bigamist George Reynolds trying to be "a law unto himself," the principle in the *Yoder* case was that subjecting him and his children to the state compulsory attendance law would require "state interests of the highest order"—interests that could not be served otherwise—before they could "overbalance legitimate claims to the free exercise of religion."[15] This seemed a world away from the *Reynolds* premise that a law is a law and that *actions* contrary to law are punishable notwithstanding the protected right to *believe* as one will.

Justice Douglas, usually a noted libertarian on the Court, wrote a dissenting opinion. His disagreement reflected the fact that one of the reasons for law's complications is life's complications. He did not differ with the view that, as the majority said, the state must show a "compelling interest" before it may suppress freedom of action prompted by religious principles. Instead, the Douglas dissent reflected his view that the Amish insistence on no more than an eighth-grade education invaded rights—certainly, arguable rights—of the Amish children. He mentioned that a lower-court judge, dissenting from the decision favoring Yoder, had questioned the picture of Amish "idyllic agrarianism."[16] Without tarrying over that, he opined that the children should be heard before the parental power over their schooling was sustained. The majority observed that no child had asked to be heard, leaving this possible issue for some other day that as yet does not appear to have come. But that, if more than a little arresting and bemusing, is not at the very center of our subject.

The center, as it was marked in *Yoder*, was the idea of a strong—a "compelling"—state interest as a requirement for suppressing or punishing actions driven by sincere religious beliefs. That certainly leaves intact the power of the state to forbid human sacrifice, the destruction of other people's property, driving on the wrong side of the road, perhaps even bigamy, among many other things. But it makes clear at the same time that some wide, if unpredictable, leeway is left for being exempted from general laws that apply to others if your religious principles call out for the exemption and no overriding interest of the government requires that you conform. That at least was true for the Yoder family. It had also been true beginning a decade earlier for a number of people claiming unemployment compensation in the face of laws disentitling people who refused to take available jobs.

In a 1963 case that several members of the Court found especially perplexing, it was held that a South Carolina Seventh-Day Adventist could not be held ineligible for unemployment compensation when she quit a job requiring her to work on Saturdays and refused to take a new job where there was the same requirement.[17] The state law said that to receive compensation a worker had to be "available" for "suitable work" and that the refusal to qualify by agreeing to work on Saturday made her unavailable. The state could not do this, the majority ruled, because it (1) imposed a burden on the free exercise of her religion and (2) did this without justifying it by some compelling interest. Though it probably remains, as lawyers say, good law, the decision did not answer to everyone's satisfaction some of the nice questions raised by both concurring and dissenting Justices and by some scholarly critics.

The questioners stressed as a basic issue that the Court was granting an *exception* on religious grounds and that this favoring of a religious claim could be assailed as a violation of the Establishment Clause. Why, for instance, wouldn't South Carolina have to make a similar exemption for a mother who could not work on Saturday (or some other day) because she could not get baby-sitting help? Nobody suggested that South Carolina would have to do this. But then must religion be favored by the state over motherhood? And in the face of the Establishment Clause forbidding government to favor religion? The majority found it a sufficient answer that requiring the Seventh-Day Adventist to work on her Sabbath or lose unemployment compensation placed a *burden* on her free exercise of religion. The majority might have observed, but it was probably just as well that it did not, that the Constitution puts no impediment against the state's placing burdens on the free exercise of motherhood. (If you've noticed with interest that the Court put this hypothetical in terms of mothers, not *parents* generally, you'll realize that this was way back in 1963—and then that the realistic question hasn't changed too dramatically—but that, too, is an aside barely finding its way into a parenthesis.)

The issues that the Court majority did not answer to everyone's satisfaction multiplied as one went through the several opinions. In the course of his opinion for the Court, Justice Brennan mentioned almost as a throwaway that South Carolina imposed no requirement on Sunday worshippers similar to that on the Sabbatarian. That, the Justice wrote, "compounded" the unconstitutionality of the Sabbatarian's treatment. One might have imagined that this, rather than simply "compounding," could serve as the heart of the decision, since government favoritism for the majority religion was a principal evil against which the First Amendment was directed. Still, with none of the nine Justices voting for that route, it must have contained bumps or barriers that do not leap instantly to my eye.

A more formidable doubt about the unemployment compensation decision stemmed from the cases just two years earlier in which the Court had upheld state *criminal* laws requiring merchants to keep their stores closed on Sundays even if they were Jews or others who observed some different day as their Sabbath.[18] The protesting storekeepers complained that these laws put them at a competitive disadvantage, requiring them to stay closed two days of the week to conform to both the state law and their religious principles.

Some argued, and it was not disputed, that the disadvantage might wipe out their businesses, a burden not lighter than the lost twenty-two weeks of unemployment compensation that was to be found unacceptable two years later. The Court, though divided, found a sufficiently compelling state interest in a uniform day of rest and upheld the Sunday-closing laws on that basis. That rationale never pleased everyone, including the dissenting Justices. It looked less imposing a couple of decades later when the shopping malls of suburbia, and then many of the central city stores, were discovered to be bustling and money-changing seven days a week. Still, to paraphrase what Thurgood Marshall suggested for his epitaph, the Justices presumably do the best they can with what they have at the given time of their lives. It was not long, in any event, before the Sunday-closing laws yielded to the pressures of commerce, generating new questions under the First Amendment.

If the legislatures are normally forbidden to burden people in their observance of a Sabbath that is different from the majority's, would it not raise respect for the Constitution to new heights if the law required employers to respect any employee's Sabbath, whatever it might be? Connecticut's legislature apparently thought so. It passed a law giving every worker the right to state any day as his or her Sabbath and forbidding employers to fire anyone for refusing to work on that day. Donald Thornton, a managerial employee of Caldor's retail stores, was a Presbyterian who observed *Sunday* as his Sabbath. Transferred and demoted for that, he brought a proceeding for back pay and other relief. Caldor's defense, among other things, attacked the Sabbath-selection law as unconstitutional. The Connecticut supreme court agreed with Caldor, and the U.S. Supreme Court sustained that position.[19]

Agreeing with the Connecticut high court, the U.S. Court (voting 8–1, with Justice Rehnquist dissenting but writing no opinion) found that the Connecticut law violated the Establishment Clause because it had the impermissible primary effect of advancing religion. Employees were empowered to ride roughshod over all other related interests in enforcing their individual Sabbath choices—for example, the interests of employers and of other employees who were not Sabbath observers. No adjustment was made where a high percentage of employees chose the same Sabbath. The opinion striking down the law was short, and seemed simple. The open-and-shut appearance is often the way with cases embalmed in the books. So it is worth recalling that a number of organizations identified with both branches of the First Amendment, the Free Exercise and the Establishment Clauses, filed briefs *amicus curiae* urging that the Connecticut statute be upheld. Still, the decision seems to be solidly grounded after all in the view of the great Judge Learned Hand, quoted in the opinion that no one has or should be given a right under the First Amendment to make others "conform their conduct to his own religious necessities."

At most an interesting qualifier of the Sabbath observer's rights, that *Caldor* decision did not strike anyone as a bombshell. A far more stunning ruling was written in 1990 by Justice Scalia, in a case called *Employment Division v. Smith*,[20] holding that the Free Exercise Clause does not prevent a state from denying unemployment compensation to workers fired from their drug rehabilitation jobs for misconduct when they used peyote as part of the ceremonies of the Native American Church in which they participated as a matter of sincerely held religious beliefs. The bombshell in the case was less what it decided than the explanation given in the opinion—a subject we will get to in a moment. But the ruling itself was more than a little unsettling.

Nobody had ever had a test case about the use of sacramental wine during Prohibition days; the lawmakers had made exceptions for the mainstream religions. A number of states made similar exceptions for peyote, so no cases came from them to the Supreme Court. But Oregon made no exception, and now the Court found no basis in the First Amendment for exempting the peyote users. One has an uneasy feeling that a different answer might have been found for a Roman Catholic or Anglican or Jewish ceremony employing fermented grapes. Is alcohol that different from peyote? Or are the relevant differences those generally between the Native American Church and the more familiar ones? Is it perhaps some of each, with the qualities of strangeness, and therefore deviance, reinforcing each other? Thoughts like these, whether put bluntly or more subtly, suggest a premise to which we'll return: that maybe a key, for courts and for all of us, is in a First Amendment use of the golden rule, testing the alien and the suspect by the same standards as those we would apply to cozier, more familiar things.

The more unsettling aspect of the peyote decision was the sweeping abandonment of the "compelling government interest" test for denying an exemption from general criminal laws for religiously driven conduct. This is perhaps an excessively unqualified statement of what the Court did. Justice Scalia, writing with his considerable skill for the majority, made a case for the position that the quoted test had never been followed anyhow except in very limited and distinguishable circumstances. The subtleties of his position, which has drawn a hail of scholarly criticism, are too much to cope with here. It is enough, and probably fair enough, to say his opinion seemed to travel most of the way back to the bigamy case of George Reynolds, which he cited repeatedly and seemed to follow as authoritative.

One among other interesting postscripts to the *Smith* decision: In June 1991, having gotten the green light to punish religious users of peyote, the Oregon legislature passed a statute forgoing that pleasure. Under the law, except for people in prison, it is now lawful to use peyote in connection "with the good faith practice of a religious belief" or association "with a religious practice."[21]

The enactment is a reminder of an important point: the U.S. Supreme Court sets *minimum* standards of freedom, but nothing stops others who exercise state power from doing better than the minimum. The legislature, elected to represent all the people, is a key place in which to remember and implement this principle. Increasingly in recent years, the state courts have also been doing better than the Supreme Court on the freedom front.

It turned out, moreover, that the return to a less liberal past was short-lived for a far wider group, the U.S. Congress. Justice Scalia's opinion had triggered an explosion of protest across a wide spectrum of religious and other organizations devoted to a generous view of the Free Exercise Clause. The result was the Religious Freedom Restoration Act of 1993, which revives as a matter of statute the rule that

> Government may substantially burden a person's exercise of religion only if it demonstrates that application of the burden to the person—
> (1) is in furtherance of a compelling governmental interest; and
> (2) is the least restrictive means of furthering that compelling governmental interest.

The result is to return the law in this respect to what it was before Justice Scalia's *Smith* decision.

There are arguments about whether Congress has the power to reverse the Supreme Court in this fashion. The arguments are not frivolous and they are too complex to handle in a book like this one. I dare, however, to opine that the statute will stand and that the "restoration" decreed by Congress will be an effective happy ending to this particular segment of constitutional history.

Meanwhile, the Court had already demonstrated earlier in 1993 that its basic commitment to religious freedom remained essentially hale and hearty. The occasion was a unanimous decision (though with four opinions) striking down a barrage of four Hialeah, Florida, ordinances aimed at outlawing animal sacrifice by the Santería Church.[22] Originating in Cuba in the nineteenth century, the Santería religion is a syncretic faith of the Yoruba people brought as slaves from East Africa to Cuba. The religion merges substantial elements of Roman Catholicism into the religion imported from Africa. Among its elements is a practice of animal sacrifice; the animals that pay for these rituals include pigeons, chickens, doves, goats, sheep, and turtles among others. When the Santería Church of the Lukumi Babalu Aye announced plans to establish a house of worship in Hialeah, the city council proceeded swiftly to block its practice of animal sacrifices.

Like so many dramas played out in the Supreme Court, this one was less simple than the unanimous result might suggest. While the sacrificed animals are cooked and eaten, it appears highly probable that many of them might survive if it were not for their ritual roles. The record of the case also indicates that they are left in cruel and frightening conditions while they await destruction. There were clearly enough of such factors in the case to bring forth a large number of briefs from organizations devoted to animal welfare arguing against the church. But the decisive aspect was the fact that the city fathers, shedding highly selective tears for the animals, had taken dead aim at the Santería Church. Neither Hialeah nor the state of Florida as a whole undertook to ban hunting or fishing, whether for sustenance or for recreation. The use of live rabbits to train greyhounds for racing is condoned under the same state law that Florida's attorney general found suitable for attacking Santería. There was ample other evidence for concluding that the Hialeah ordinances targeted Santería conduct for peculiarly adverse treatment. The Court recalled that such laws can only very rarely, if ever, survive attacks under the First Amendment.

So in the term ending in June 1993, the Supreme Court

reaffirmed that government, "even in pursuit of legitimate interests, cannot in a selective manner impose burdens only on conduct motivated by religious belief." This left three Justices and many other critics dissatisfied with the sweeping statements in the peyote case denying exceptions from *general* laws (not aimed at religion) for people whose religion calls out for exceptions, whether for unemployment compensation, the education of their children, or the sacramental use of drugs like peyote or alcohol. But that concern may have been alleviated or eliminated by the Religious Freedom Restoration Act, discussed above.

In any case, things are not too bad. Decisions like that in the Santería case remind us of a regime of church-state relationships fairly realizing much of what the founders must have been dreaming about. The peroration of the majority opinion is a comforting reassurance:

> The Free Exercise Clause commits government itself to religious tolerance, and upon slight suspicion that proposals for state intervention stem from animosity to religion or distrust of its practices, all officials must pause to remember their own high duty to the Constitution and to the rights it secures. Those in office must be resolute in resisting importunate demands and must ensure that the sole reasons for imposing the burdens of law and regulation are secular. Legislators may not devise mechanisms, overt or disguised, designed to persecute or oppress a religion or its practices.

6

PROPHETS AND

PROFITEERS

Among the most inspired and familiar of passages in the volumes of Supreme Court decisions is that written for the Court by Justice Robert Jackson in the 1943 case holding the state powerless to punish Jehovah's Witnesses children and their parents for refusal to join in the schoolroom salute to the flag:

> If there is any fixed star in our constitutional constellation, it is that no official, high or petty, can prescribe what shall be orthodox in politics, nationalism, religion, or other matters of opinion or force citizens to confess by word or act their faith therein. If there are any circumstances which permit an exception, they do not now occur to us.[1]

That opinion as a whole spoke broadly of the sweep of the First Amendment rather than focusing strictly on the Religion

Clauses. But that strengthens rather than weakens it. The result is a nice reminder of why the parts of the Amendment—religion, speech, press, association—are found together, in a pattern of protections for the conscience of free people. As the Court said, its decision was designed to safeguard "the sphere of intellect and spirit which it is the purpose of the First Amendment to our Constitution to reserve from all official control."

As we observed earlier, that flag-salute case overturned a Supreme Court precedent only three years old that had held the state *was* empowered to punish refusals to participate. That brief chapter of legal history epitomizes what may fairly be described as the "price" members of the community must be ready to pay for religious freedom. Experience through the ages reflects the powerful urge most of us feel to compel acceptance by others of our deepest and most significant beliefs. In most places and at most times, at least until very recently, that sentiment has made life difficult and risky for nonconformists. People who question the established ideas are seen to be dangerous, as they sometimes are. The deviant is a threat and a challenge. The things we hold sacred must be respected, and rejection is a form of disrespect. Moreover, if our fundamental beliefs are questioned or denied, unless we hold them with a certainty that is not universal, we may begin to doubt them ourselves, and that can be profoundly disturbing. However we account for it, the impulse to compel conformity has been a powerful one. The First Amendment, countering that drive, carries tension as part of its cost.

That tension is a virtually inescapable consequence of the fact that differences and conflicts in religious beliefs are in their nature irreconcilable. Built on faith in what cannot be seen or demonstrated, they are at the same time priceless and unquestionable for millions of adherents. Differences of opinion at this level can be, and too often have been, fatal. Did God, if there is a God, talk to Moses? Was Jesus the Son of God, descended from an Immaculate Conception? Was the

Book of Mormon contained in the golden tablets revealed to Joseph Smith at Palmyra, New York? Was Muhammad selected by God to be the Arab prophet of true religion? Is it true, as Christian Science teaches, that the material world is all an illusion and that faith rather than medicine is the way to defeat sickness? Questions like these can be multiplied almost endlessly if we examine the hundreds of religions in the United States and the thousands around the world. Every one of them was new once—a sect or a cult, if you like—and a target of scorn or repression. New sects or cults continue to appear. Are all or any of them "true"?

Even to ask questions like the ones in the preceding paragraph is likely to raise hackles. Especially for members of the established religions, it verges on sacrilege to ask about their eternal verities in breaths adjoining those used for comparable questions about new, alien, strange, and therefore suspect religions. Untold millions of people have been killed for doubting the revelations of others. When the power of the state has been allied with religion, the killings have been commonly the work of government officers.

Among the marvels of life in the United States is the fact that religions so numerous and varied (one encyclopedia counted 1,347 in 1987) reside together in peace. We've looked at this miracle earlier and noted that it is not fairly explained on the ground that nobody cares very much. Millions, probably a majority of us, care deeply. But the commitment to religious freedom, thus far at least, runs no less deeply, for reasons I don't claim to reckon adequately. And the First Amendment, unlike too many other things lawyers administer, serves vitally to keep that commitment strong.

Among the supreme values of the First Amendment is the principle that the discovery or declaration of religious truth is no business of government. That means, as a tautology, that the state is without power to pursue religious fraud or fakery. This is among the several junctures at which we see components of the price paid for the freedom. Religion is in its essential nature a realm of mystery, of reaches beyond human understanding, of propositions that transcend mundane proofs—of faith. It deals with our greatest perplexities, doubts, and fears. It is, therefore, of incalculable value. But it is by the same token a fertile field for fraud and fakery.

Fooling people with false answers to our ultimate questions is surely among the most odious of crimes. All decent people must yearn for the punishment of miscreants who could perpetrate wrongs of this nature. It seems pretty clear, nevertheless, that the First Amendment largely disables the government from attempting to expose or silence supposedly false prophets. That, on reflection, is about the way it should be. Though all of us could name the Elmer Gantrys we'd recommend for prosecution, we would never agree on the candidates. What is more crucial, today's charlatan may be tomorrow's saint. The believers in every religion, whether a minute few or a worldwide mass, always have arrayed against them the rest of the world, the "disbelievers." The government's central commitment under the First Amendment is neutrality.

A leading illustration of the commitment was given by the Supreme Court in 1944 in a criminal prosecution called *United States v. Ballard.*[2] It involved the I Am movement, founded by Guy Ballard. Ballard enlisted all who would listen to hear that in 1930, when he was fifty-two, he had experienced miraculous communions on Mount Shasta, California. Evidently prepared for these happenings by earlier travels in Asia, he had previously heard stories of this peak. Having prayed to God for guidance, he proceeded to climb. Along the way, he recounted, he met a young man who gave him a "creamy liquid" that turned out to be a "much more refreshing drink than spring water." The drink, the young man said, was "from the Universal Supply, pure and unifying as Life Itself." In fact, it was "Life—Omnipresent Life," Ballard was told, which "exists everywhere about us." Ballard reported other details of this encounter, and said that the young man was succeeded by Master St. Germain, who appeared before him "in a white, jeweled robe." St. Germain told him of further mysteries and took him back into earlier times in Ballard's life or lives, including an occasion when Ballard was a woman singing to the Queen of France, and a time still more remote when he was an assistant priest at a temple in Luxor. There, Ballard's wife was a vestal virgin and his son the high priest.

Ballard told of many other fabulous encounters and spiritual revelations. He published a book and a magazine. He changed his name to Godfre Ray King. His wife became Lotus. He created classes for instruction and designated group leaders. In the course of a decade followers of the I Am movement were to be found across the entire United States. Financial support came in a variety of forms, including contributions and the proceeds of sales of religious objects. One such item was an engraving portraying Jesus, sketched by a high leader of the movement who reported having seen Jesus in 1935 and portrayed what he had seen on the engraving. The engraving sold for two dollars for a 12 × 16-inch size and fifty cents for a 5 × 7-inch version.

After Ballard's death in 1939, the movement was carried on by his widow and his son. In 1940 they and a number of leadership colleagues were charged in a federal indictment that appears to have destroyed the movement even though the indictment was dropped after convictions were twice reversed by the Supreme Court and finally set aside for a trial error that is not pertinent here. The indictment was for mail fraud, the prosecution charging that the Ballards had taken in over $3 million in the years 1930–40 by means of false representations as to St. Germain and their claimed power to heal illness by religious intervention. The decision on the first appeal bears on our subject.

In that appeal, without reaching the question that later

invalidated the convictions, a bare majority of five laid down
the rule that appears to have prevailed in succeeding years—
that the truth or falsity of religious affirmations is not a permissible subject for the secular courts. In so holding, the Court
sustained the trial judge, who had instructed the jury that the
Ballards' *sincerity*, but not the truth of what they said, was
a material factor. (Since the indictment had charged *falsity*
and the defendants had been prevented from proving that
what they said was true, the technical correctness of the holding by both the trial judge and the Supreme Court could be
debated, but that is now a forgotten detail.) In ruling that
religious truth is none of the government's business, Justice
Douglas wrote eloquently for the majority:

> Heresy trials are foreign to our Constitution. Men may
> believe what they cannot prove. They may not be put to
> the proof of their religious doctrines or beliefs. Religious
> experiences which are as real as life to some may be incom-
> prehensible to others. Yet the fact that they may be beyond
> the ken of mortals does not mean that they can be made
> suspect before the law. Many take their gospel from the
> New Testament. But it would hardly be supposed that they
> could be tried before a jury charged with the duty of de-
> termining whether those teachings contained false repre-
> sentations. The miracles of the New Testament, the Divinity
> of Christ, life after death, the power of prayer are deep in
> the religious convictions of many. If one could be sent to
> jail because a jury in a hostile environment found those
> teachings false, little indeed would be left of religious free-
> dom. The Fathers of the Constitution were not unaware of
> the varied and extreme views of religious sects, of the vi-
> olence of disagreement among them, and of the lack of any
> one religious creed on which all men would agree. They
> fashioned a charter of government which envisaged the wid-
> est possible toleration of conflicting views. Man's relation
> to his God was made no concern of the state. He was granted

the right to worship as he pleased and to answer to no man
for the verity of his religious views.[3]

Justice Harlan Stone, joined by two others, was "not prepared to say that the constitutional guaranty of freedom of
religion affords immunity from criminal prosecution for the
fraudulent procurement of money by false statements as to
one's religious experiences." He proposed as hypothetical
cases a defendant's claim that he'd shaken St. Germain's hand
in San Francisco when the defendant had never been in that
city or a claim of cured diseases refuted by evidence that there
had been no cures.

Justice Douglas could not resist an observation that the
views "espoused by [the Ballards] might seem incredible,
if not preposterous, to most people." Possibly in strictest
logic, if the truth of those views was, as Douglas said, a "forbidden domain" for American officials, speculation about
what "most people" might think had no place in the opinion.
But however minutely precise we could want to be about that,
the point was clearly made. In fact, it may be all the clearer
for the reminder that it is the far-out and generally rejected
notion that most requires protection in the realm of religion.
Like other hypotheticals that members of the legal profession
find useful (not, it should be said, without some justification),
Justice Stone's suggested cases of fraud by fake religionists
are not unpersuasive. They have not been influential, however,
perhaps because the kinds of literal falsehoods they described
are not in fact used by actual wrongdoers. Prosecutors have
in any event not pursued these types of claims.

Justice Jackson stood alone, dissenting. He started his opinion with observations that the Ballards might not have found
undilutedly cheering:

If I might agree to their conviction without creating a precedent, I cheerfully would do so. I can see in their teachings

nothing but humbug, untainted by any trace of truth. But that does not dispose of the constitutional question whether misrepresentation of religious experience or belief is prosecutable; it rather emphasizes the danger of such prosecutions.

Expanding on that conclusion, he would have ruled that alleged insincerity was no more proper than falsity as a subject for prosecuting claims of religious fraud. The best proof of sincerity, he argued, was proof of the *truth* of the asserted experiences, which the majority was ruling immaterial. Furthermore, he said, religious experiences lie in a realm of mystery, of the unseen, of visions, and of uniquely personal sensation—qualities that a jury ought not to be free to examine or to deny at a defendant's risk of imprisonment. And how, after all, could courts and juries competently identify or measure sincerity? How to appraise or measure the alleged adherent who takes the Bible literally as against one who reads it as allegory? What of the minister who has "lost the faith" but continues to preach and to minister? The task of separating the fake from the sincere was, in Justice Jackson's view, too chancy and dangerous to be given to judges and jurors. He might perhaps have invoked the wag who said if you can fake sincerity, you've really got it made.

There is much that is obviously sound and persuasive in Justice Jackson's dissent. While he won no votes on the Supreme Court, his views seem to have carried weight in the practical legal world. Prosecutions for religious fraud remain rarities, as they probably should, giving religious freedom the wide berth that is desirable if the freedom is to remain clear and robust.

This does not signify that fraud in religious trappings is always and everywhere immune from detection in the courthouse or the city streets. The chinks in the armor of religious pretenders who prey on faith to defraud believers become permeable when concrete lies are detected and the purses of followers are invaded by frauds that have nothing to do with asserted religious beliefs.

When the televangelist promises to intercede with God for followers who send a small contribution, the law is probably powerless to intervene and try to demonstrate beyond a reasonable doubt that the promised communications did not happen. The same is even clearer where the spiritual leader makes no such relatively specific promise but merely solicits money to keep the church well enough heeled to have its leadership live as lushly as some of God's anointed messengers appear to deem suitable. But some kinds of false representations are detectable without trenching at all on the realm of the spirit, and scams of this kind can lead to jail cells for rapacious pseudo-seers.

For instance, *Newsweek* magazine for April 6, 1987, featured on its cover a garish photo of Jim and Tammy Bakker next to a headline that said: "Holy Wars—Money, Sex and Power." The story inside the magazine was headed "God and Money." It reported a prior year's income of $129 million for the Bakker ministry, headquartered on a 2,300-acre theme park, Heritage USA, in Fort Mill, South Carolina. One of the other featured preachers, Jimmy Swaggart, had taken in $142 million in the preceding year and was said to have 1,000 employees, a TV recording studio, and the Jimmy Swaggart Bible College, among other properties. Swaggart was later to fall a ways, and then perhaps to recover, because of some sexual misbehavior and so is outside the present account.

Bakker, however, was moved from his lush PTL ("Praise the Lord") ministry to a long sojourn in a federal prison following his conviction for large-scale garden-variety fraud that had nothing to do with his professed religious teachings. Briefly, the fraud consisted of selling "lifetime partnerships" at prices ranging from $500 to $10,000, many bought with the life savings of his followers, entitling the purchasers to annual sojourns at his Heritage Village. One bald species of fraud was his representation that he'd sell only 25,000 of these so that there would be room for the buyers when he then went ahead and sold more than 66,000. Even at that, instead of his using the money to build the promised lodgings, much of it, as a federal court of appeals said, went "to support a lavish lifestyle" that included "gold-plated fixtures and a $570 shower curtain in his bathroom, transportation in private jets and limousines, an air-conditioned treehouse for his children and an air-conditioned doghouse for his pets."[4] Whatever the judges or jury may have thought privately, the conviction had nothing to do with anybody's views on how well Bakker's way of life comported with the Christianity he preached, or even with questions of his sincerity. The frauds for which he was convicted could have been those of any other swindler running amok with money extracted under false pretenses.

It is not surprising or disturbing that frauds like Bakker's should be punishable wholly without regard to clerical garb or religious teachings. The most devout of preachers are expected to report and pay tax on their incomes, just as they must obey speed limits, the laws against child molestation, and other rules that do not implicate their religious beliefs or teachings. To be sure, the lines that seem easy to draw get fuzzy in this quarter, as in others, when the varieties of both religious and legal experience are confronted.

A closer case than Bakker's was that of the Reverend Sun Myung Moon, head of the American branch of the Unification Church (sometimes irreverently known as the "Moonies"), convicted in 1982 of filing false federal tax returns and sentenced to eighteen months in prison. On the appeal from that conviction, argued by distinguished counsel and supported by a number of civil liberties and religious organizations, the federal court of appeals observed near the outset of its lengthy opinion that the defense raised "troubling issues of religious persecution and abridgement of free speech."[5] The conviction was affirmed, however, despite the evident substantiality of the issues.

Moon argued, among other things, that his Korean ancestry had led to his being singled out for a prosecution that would not have happened to a Western minister of one of the better-established religions. In the same vein, he complained that the trial court had wrongly denied him the opportunity to be tried *without* a jury, the plausible thought being that his race and nonmainstream religion could well have evoked undetectable juror biases less likely to infect the trial judge alone. More central to the doctrine we've been looking at was an argument on the key tax question—whether a large bank account from which he had paid substantial personal expenses should have been deemed his, so that he owed taxes on the interest income, or that of his church, as he claimed. Moon's position, in a word, was that the account was hold in trust for the church for "religious purposes." When the jury was permitted to find against him on that, an evident basis for the conviction, his counsel argued that the First Amendment was violated. It was not for a lay jury, they said, to consider what were religious purposes. If the expenditures for personal things by the top leader were for religious purposes under the definition of the Unification Church, that should have been the end of the matter.

The court's rejection of that position seems sound, but hardly beyond the realm of debate. Without dwelling more on the details of the legal position, it remains of interest that some forty religious individuals and organizations—including the Presbyterians (U.S.A.), the American Baptist Churches in the United States, the Catholic League for Religious and Civil Rights, and the Church of Jesus Christ of Latter-Day Saints —supported his unsuccessful petition to have the Supreme Court review the case.

The possibly substantial issue as to what expenses are "personal" and what "religious" can be carried of course to absurd extremes. That appears to have happened in a number of essentially trivial cases in which people have undertaken to manipulate the law, including the Constitution, by setting themselves up as "churches" or tax-exempt "religions" as a means of evading taxes. The cases are not legion, but numerous enough to be disgusting. And they run to a pattern suggesting that some warped petty larcenist has distributed, perhaps sold, the worthless formula. The idea, very simply, is for some seemingly ordinary taxpayer—a truck driver, an engineer, a computer operator, for examples—to set himself or herself up as a "church," serving as minister, deacon, and congregation all in one. The unimaginative cheat then takes a vow of poverty, asserts that all his or her income is that of the church, uses the income in the usual way for personal things, and claims it is all tax-exempt. The device is about as effective as is the slender tree on the opera stage to hide the corpulent diva. But the tax authorities are unwilling to suspend disbelief, and sooner or later descend with assessments, search warrants, even criminal prosecutions in egregious cases.

Unedifying attempts of that sort are interesting only as sociology. They do not illuminate or reflect the unending stream of genuinely challenging problems that arise as we try to protect both the freedom of religion and the potential victims of those who would use religion as a cloak for shell games. When a sharp choice must be made, Justice Jackson's approach continues to be appealing: the people must be on guard for themselves against religious fraud if the only alternative is to have government as the arbiter of religious truth. There is steady pressure, nevertheless, to enlist the force of the state against possible abuses of the trust people are led to repose on account of their religious faith. And the result is a continuing series of close, perplexing cases.

One of these involved what does not appear at first blush

to be a deeply spiritual question, the regulation of kosher food sales. For observant Jews, it is a vital requirement that their food be kosher—meaning, among other things, that it be within prescribed food categories and, specifically, that meats be only from specified parts of particular animals, slaughtered and prepared according to stated rules. To complicate the subject, different groups within Judaism have disagreements as to the rules. While there are differences over the specifics, there is no question that compliance with the requirements is labor intensive, so that kosher foods tend to cost more than nonkosher foods. The result is an opportunity for the unscrupulous to pass off nonkosher food as kosher, which can lead to a variety of injuries, even to health. (For example, since shellfish is a forbidden category, people with allergies, including non-Jews, buy kosher fish products to avoid risk.)

To guard against frauds of this nature, New Jersey's Division of Consumer Affairs adopted regulations making it an "unlawful consumer practice" to sell food "falsely represented to be Kosher." The regulations defined "kosher" to mean "prepared and maintained in strict compliance with the laws and customs of the Orthodox Jewish religion." The regulations went on to provide guidelines for kosher meats, dealing with such matters as washing, deveining, and separate storage. A Bureau of Kosher Enforcement was established within the division. The attorney general created a state Kosher Advisory Committee composed of ten rabbis to advise on enforcement and consider needed changes.

By a vote of 4–3 the New Jersey Supreme Court in 1992 held that regulatory apparatus unconstitutional.[6] It created, as the majority saw it, an unacceptable degree of entanglement between the state and religion, violating the Establishment Clause. Lengthy opinions, going both ways, reflected that the question was not an easy one. Regulatory arrangements of a similar nature had been upheld in a number of other states.

And the basic purpose—to prevent or punish fraud—was sound.

For all that, the decision seems wise. It leaves open other, agreed, neutral means of defining "kosher" without the involvement of state officials in deciding what is "Orthodox" and what arguable details may pass muster. It eliminates the spectacle of ten members of the clergy serving as a state advisory committee. And it is a salutary reminder that defining religious correctness is not acceptable work for government agencies. The religious community can and should muster means of its own, independent of government, for policing compliance with kosher food regulations. The fact that public officials might be more effective because they are more powerful is not a sufficient reason for enlisting them. The price in intermingled religion and government is too high.

That sort of conclusion will remain debatable. For myself, I would continue to vote with Justice Jackson. At a minimum, the close cases should be decided for freedom, leaving the Elmer Gantrys at large even while we imprison the Jim Bakkers.

7

RELIGIOUS
SCHOOLS AND GOVERNMENT
MONEY

As noted in Chapter 1, the school-bus case of *Everson* in 1947 is the springboard for modern American constitutional law on church and state. For many lawyers and others who care about the subject, the fact that the case was decided on a 5–4 vote has been a source of frustrated handwringing. How can such great issues and the underlying tension be resolved by such hairline differences in the vote? With the passage of time, however, and the experience of the intervening half century, the sharp 1947 division on the Court seems less important than the wide area of agreement, both in *Everson* itself and in the cases of later years. In fact, the nine Justices of 1947 may be seen in retrospect to have been more unanimous than their successors on fundamentals like Jefferson's wall of separation.

It is fairly arguable that 5–4 votes happen only when the

cloudy boundaries are being set—as, say, where the line needs to be drawn between safe bus rides for little children and the ban against state money for religious groups—whereas the wide center of agreement on the basics is unanimous. If that may be less than exactly so, there is no room to doubt that the task of line drawing with respect to schools has been the most prolific and vexing of church-state subjects. Floods of scholarly and judicial ink have been loosed on "parochaid," as this problem is labeled by some of the debaters. The subject is addressed by more Supreme Court cases than any other single category. While the stream is not steady, it appears to be endless. A confluence of strong and persistent forces promises to keep the topic a live one.

The battleground is one of the blessings we tend to take for granted—the institution of free, public, *secular* education. As history goes, this is a recent innovation. For most of our ancestral past, education was a private affair, principally for the aristocracy and largely purveyed by private tutors. Wider forms were tied to religion—in the monasteries and then in church schools. Protestantism, stressing the direct access of every adherent to Holy Writ, enhanced the call for literacy, tying both the demand and the supply to churches. Though Jefferson, once again in the creative vanguard, taught the need for public and secular education, it was some time before the idea was implemented across the nation. But it was of course adopted. Undoubtedly propelled by the growing needs of industry for a literate work force, among other causes, free public education took root first in New England and spread from there to the rest of the country. By the last quarter of the nineteenth century, public schools separate from the churches were found everywhere.

The course of this development, like others, was neither smooth nor unopposed. Roman Catholics were, and have remained, skeptical or hostile toward the idea of public education. Until well into the twentieth century, while the United

States was as a practical matter run by white Protestants, a vital ground of Catholic concern was the presence in the public schools of sectarian Protestant influences, notably the King James Bible reading that Catholic children and their parents resisted against strong and sometimes abusive pressure. As the Protestant hegemony waned, Catholic skepticism toward public education, and especially toward the tax burden it entails, has not disappeared, though it has abated.

The main impetus for dispute is the fact that in the Catholic philosophy the idea of education divorced from religion is incongruous and unacceptable in principle. In the Catholic parochial school, the paramount spirit and concepts of religion pervade the curriculum. For the Catholic Church, the sound educational arrangement is the parochial school, with each denomination in charge of the schools for children of its faith.

As an incident of this position, it is experienced as a galling burden for Catholics to be taxed for public secular schools while they must then pay in addition for the running of their religious schools as private enterprises. This has meant over the decades a steady campaign to seek public money for at least a substantial portion (the supposedly secular portion, supposedly separable) of the parochial-school cost. Failing that, the aim is public funding for as many aspects of parochial-school education as possible—for special education of the handicapped, for secular texts and materials used by both public and private schools, for religiously neutral equipment, and for whatever other subventions can be formulated as being different from public support of the religious organization. These pressures are abetted by other parochial-school groups—including Orthodox Jews and Lutherans. But the preponderant leadership remains Roman Catholic.

The quest for "indirect" or partial economic assistance remains essentially a kind of second-best or sideshow position. The principal sentiment has been and remains a grievance against the inequity, as it is seen, of requiring Catholics to support the public schools for other people's children while they must bear the duplicative burden of maintaining their own schools. A distinguished prelate and political philosopher, Father John Courtney Murray, argued bitterly against the "anomaly" of denying public money to parochial schools.[1] There is no anomaly, of course, under the essential principles of church-state separation as defined for this purpose by Madison, Jefferson, and the Supreme Court in the twentieth century. But for Father Murray and the major spokesmen of the Catholic Church, those principles are wrong and unacceptable. Very much in the mainstream of the Court's doctrine on other subjects (for example, the school desegregation decision of 1954), Father Murray inveighed in strong terms against Madison's "absolutism," as he saw it, and the "particular rigid, radical, and absolute" doctrine laid down in the *Everson* case—both Madison and the *Everson* decision amounting to an "irredeemable piece of sectarian dogmatism" that is "demonstrably false" and scarcely rescued by being a "deistic version of fundamentalist Protestantism."[2]

For all that feisty eloquence, and for all his undoubtedly virtuous leadership in other respects, Father Murray was and remains desperately mistaken in my view and, more important, in the substantially unanimous view of the Supreme Court. There are small qualifications of that basic position, to be sure, as every sweeping proposition needs some flexibility in a living system of law, and we'll observe the qualifications in a little while. Nevertheless, the position stands, and it ought to. It has served the nation well. It has guarded against the divisive struggles among religions at the public trough that would follow for sure from the regime of public finance for religion against which Madison waged his successful battles. The demand of churches for public money reflects in the end a deep ignorance or repudiation of the most vital premises of the Religion Clauses.

The essence of the wall of separation carried forward by Madison and Jefferson from Roger Williams and embodied in the Constitution meant above everything else that the new democracy was to refrain from giving money to support any church or all churches. Madison had made it plain in his successful Virginia campaigns that led to the First Amendment that the barrier was meant to prevent government from forcing anyone to support even his or her own church. The prohibition was to remain absolute and total. In his famous resistance to assessments by government for any or all churches he spoke out against even trivial exactions—of "three pence only"—because that would open the way in principle to the kind of enlistment of the state by religion against which he warned.

That was brilliantly sound when the great majority of all Americans were Protestant Christians, though the sectarian divisions even then counseled against inviting the churches to joust at the public fisc. The wisdom of the position has not abated as the sects have multiplied. Catholics at the moment, while far from a majority, are the largest single denomination. There is no telling, however, how long that will last. Islam is the fastest growing religion. Immigration is changing the unmelted mix of diverse Americans. It would take a special combination of childishness and bravado to predict with confidence what we will look like one hundred years hence. The best we can do now for our successors, then, is to leave them with the kind of framework for living together in peace that has held together so well for the first two hundred years.

While we think about that, after visiting with Father Murray and other Catholic leaders, it should be noted that there is not as a practical matter a single or unique Catholic position on the subject of parochaid. For one thing, as I've noted, other sponsors of parochial schools are joined in pursuit of government money. The more important point just here is that it is not "Catholics" as a monolithic force against others.

As far as the official hierarchy is concerned, the position probably is the one stated by Father Murray. Many of the congregation, however, including some with directly relevant authority, support the constitutional position Father Murray found anathematic. For notable examples, Justice Frank Murphy joined in the *Everson* opinion reaffirming the "high and impregnable" wall between church and state in which the Court also said it "could not approve the slightest breach." Justice William J. Brennan, a powerful voice for all aspects of First Amendment freedoms and the entirety of the Bill of Rights through his thirty-four years on the Supreme Court bench (1956–90), never wavered in his support of the *Everson* principle. And John F. Kennedy, if he was sometimes thought to be less than devout, wrote specially prized chapters in the history of this subject. Campaigning effectively against anti-Catholic bigotry to become the first President of his faith, he stated the unequivocal principles separating his religion from his promised performance in that office. In keeping the promise, he added a special quality of support to the principles.

Returning from the small excursion on Catholicism and church-state separation, I want to enlarge a little on the point that the denial of government money for parochial schooling is not an utterly simple legal matter. Remember that the fountainhead *Everson* case allowed funding for school buses, the stated distinction being between benefits *for the children* and support of the school. In what critics condemn as a crazily wavering line, but I tend to accept as good-faith efforts by fallible and nonuniform judges, there has been a diversity of cases and fine distinctions.

The Supreme Court has permitted the government's provision of secular textbooks to be used by parochial-school children.[3] Not long after *Everson*, in 1948 it struck down a program of released time for religious instruction when the instruction was conducted in the public schoolhouse,[4] but then, in 1952, over strong dissents, allowed released time when the students were excused for religious classes elsewhere.[5] Similarly, again with sharp divisions, the Court has disallowed programs of remedial instruction in which public-school teachers went to parochial schools to engage in secular remedial teaching,[6] but permitted such teaching away from the parochial-school premises.[7] In 1973, the Court struck down a New York statute giving various forms of grants to nonpublic schools for maintenance and repair and certain forms of tax relief to parents of non-public-school children.[8] The New York legislature had found, and the Supreme Court did not disagree, that the non-public-school enrollment, about 85 percent in church-affiliated schools, eased the burdens on public-school budgets. But this was held no answer to the Establishment Clause prohibition. In 1983, however, against strenuous dissents charging the majority with departure from its own precedents, the Court upheld a Minnesota statute allowing tax deductions for school expenses despite a showing that this benefited primarily parents of children in private schools, 95 percent of which were sectarian.[9] The dissent rejected as thin and spurious the majority's distinction of the 1973 case out of New York, but could muster only four of the nine votes.

The list of cases could be extended and the intricacies made a lot clearer than these one-line summaries. A fuller account would disclose that the distinctions among the cases vary in their persuasiveness but that the Justices are engaged in meaningful struggles when they publish their unresolved disagreements. But this is not a legal treatise. My limited effort is to sketch the nature of the manifold conflicts and to underscore the suggestion that these are the materials in our system from which the fabric of the constitutional law is woven. Risking a look of Pollyannaism, I've also suggested that the resulting product should not on the whole displease us. This last thought may draw some support from a more detailed look at a couple of cases that are recent as this is written, both again decided by closely divided courts, the U.S. Supreme and New York's highest, its court of appeals.

First the case of James Zobrest, deaf since birth, needing a sign-language interpreter to accompany him to his Roman Catholic high-school classes. While he attended public school, the school district gave him that assistance. When he moved on to the parochial high school, however, the district and state authorities ruled that paying an interpreter there would violate the Establishment Clause. In a lawsuit James and his parents urged that they were being unlawfully denied a benefit they should have under a federal law for assistance to students with disabilities. A federal district judge upheld the state authorities and was affirmed 2–1 by the Ninth Circuit Court of Appeals. The Supreme Court reversed 5–4.[10] Though judges are not fungible, it is an occasional pastime among lawyers to mark facts like the tie score of 6–6 when all the judges who looked at the case are added together. (A full account requires the additional point that only two of the four dissenting Justices went off on the Establishment Clause ground, the other two voting only that the constitutional issue, for reasons uninteresting here, should not have been reached at all.)

In the majority opinion by Chief Justice Rehnquist, the Court assimilated the case to those involving generally available benefits neutrally provided to any "broad class of citizens defined without reference to religion." The Catholic school, it held, derived no benefit from the provision of the interpreter; the handicapped child was the beneficiary. The case was distinguished from those forbidding participation of public employees in parochial-school teaching. The sign-language interpreter was viewed as a kind of religiously neutral appurtenance who would "neither add to nor subtract from" the sectarian environment in which he was assigned to assist young Mr. Zobrest.

Justice Blackmun's dissenting opinion, joined by Justice

Souter, identified the majority decision as turning "upon the distinction between a teacher and a sign-language interpreter." He observed that before this case the Court had "never . . . authorized a public employee to participate directly in religious indoctrination." He stressed the pervasiveness of religion in the Catholic school: "In an environment so pervaded by discussions of the divine, the interpreter's every gesture would be infused with religious significance." Seeing the case this way, he recalled and would have applied a 1975 decision rejecting the "fiction that a . . . program could be saved by masking it as aid to individual students."[11]

My vote, if I'd had one, would have gone with Justice Blackmun's dissent. With the question that close, the tipping factor would have been the premise that the wall of separation must be kept high and solid, with breaches for doubtful occasions being avoided. But the decision could not be—was not—an easy one. If ever a situation called for just a wee crack in the wall, the appeal of the Zobrests was in that category. Disagreeing, then, along with many others, I see no warrant for despair or cynicism in the majority's result. There is nothing in it of the implicit or unconscious religiosity that could lead a scant majority to swallow the government-sponsored crèche in Providence, Rhode Island, or prompt Justice Scalia to the expressions of devout outrage over the banning of a government-sponsored graduation prayer in the same city. It is no more pro-religion than the graduation-prayer case was anti-religion. It is simply another instance of finding the sometimes cloudy line that should separate church from state following conceptions that cannot be mechanical.

Finally, a case that divided New York's highest court 4–2 and then the U.S. Supreme Court 6–3 suggests in its unique circumstances (as well as the two majorities of two-thirds) the seemingly endless varieties of conundrums that can arise when earnestly religious people invoke the collaboration of government to further their peculiar religious needs in the education of their children. A group of Satmar Hasidic Jews, settled in a community in upstate New York, presented special difficulties in the provision of special education for those of their children who were handicapped. They formed a village, Kiryas Joel, composed almost entirely and exclusively of members of their sect. Their faith commands, among other rules of conduct, that they follow a prescribed dress code, keep the sexes separate in school and elsewhere, and in general keep separate from the outside community. The education of their nonhandicapped children has raised no issue; they attend parochial schools supported with private funds. But their desire to have the benefit of publicly funded special education for the handicapped posed legal perplexities for state and local officials over a period of years.

Finally, in 1989, they worked out an arrangement with the legislature and the governor to create a public-school district coterminous with their village of Kiryas Joel. The new district was carved out of a larger district that surrounded it. This made it possible for the Satmar Hasidim, now controlling the school board, to provide special-education services for their handicapped children in a segregated environment with public funding—the heart of the matter being, of course, the use of government money. That is to say, it *would have* been possible if the legislation had not been struck down as unconstitutional.

Two of the four-judge majority, reviewing the U.S. Supreme Court precedents, found that the prohibited principal or primary effect of the special school-district law was the advancement of religion. Two others found an extension of special privileges to a religious sect without the showing of a compelling governmental interest that might conceivably have justified that. Two dissenters would have upheld the state law as "a Solomon-like solution"—"secular, neutral and benign within the reasonable doubt spectrum"—and found the sign-language interpretation case of *Zobrest* persuasive for upholding the Hasidic school district.

The Supreme Court agreed with the New York Court of

Appeals on June 27, 1994, producing five opinions for the
majority of six and a sixth opinion by Justice Scalia dissenting
for himself, Justice Thomas, and Chief Justice Rehnquist.[12]
(Arrays of opinions like this call for sometimes intricate patch-
ing to figure out what the law is. It has been argued that they
make for something less than an "intelligible Constitution."[13]
In this *Kiryas Joel* case, for illustration, the judgment of the
Court was delivered by Justice Souter in an opinion of which
four other Justices joined in "Parts I, II-B, II-C, and III," but
only those parts, while three of those four joined in "Parts II
(introduction) and II-A." Four of the other Justices in the
majority wrote concurring opinions, agreeing on the result,
but adding to or subtracting from the Souter opinion.) A basic
proposition on which all of the majority seemed to agree is
that the special statute for Kiryas Joel was "tantamount to
an allocation of political power on a religious criterion and
neither presuppose[d] nor require[d] governmental impar-
tiality toward religion." The majority took the occasion to
reaffirm "a principle at the heart of the Establishment Clause,
that government should not prefer one religion to another,
or religion to irreligion." Justice Kennedy would have gone
on the narrower ground that the state is barred by the Establishment Clause from "drawing political boundaries on
the basis of religion."

The majority was not unmoved by the plight of the Satmar
Hasidim, whose unconventional dress, language, and other
characteristics make it specially painful for their handicapped
children to be educated along with others. Two of the majority's opinions suggested other means by which their parents
could serve their needs without transgressing the Constitution.
As this is written, in the summer of 1994, the New York
legislature has made efforts to comply that sound dubious
enough to foretell another round of appellate opinions.

All that trouble should not have been necessary in the view
of the dissenting Justices. The opinion of Justice Scalia for
these three was described as "strident" and "petulant" in a

New York Times editorial, which opined that these three members of the Court "have rarely seen a religious preference they didn't approve."[14] For all its abrasiveness, however, the dissent stirs questions that are likely to remain perplexing in the future, centering on the difficulties of drawing lines between "toleration" and "accommodation" on one hand and impermissible favoritism or religious classification on the other.

Though the case may have been difficult, like most of the few that find their way to the Supreme Court, the decision seems sound and salutary to me. A contrary precedent would have disturbing implications. The Satmar Hasidim are not the first and will not be the last of religious groups that want to be alone. It is one thing to allow full freedom for that. It is quite another to combine civic and religious authority in support of that desire. As the Supreme Court said of another statute it held unconstitutional, the Kiryas Joel law was a potential prelude to "successive opportunities for political fragmentation and division along religious lines, one of the principal evils against which the Establishment Clause was intended to protect."[15]

The New York and Washington dissenters were surely not bent on promoting scholastic monasteries or other religious communities by supplying them with school districts drawn on religious lines. But that invitation was proposed by their position. Arguably, the invitation could be withdrawn if there were many acceptances. On the other hand, the majority objected to the New York statute on the debatable ground that there was no assurance of similar treatment in the future for groups other than the Kiryas Joel parents. The best view of all may be in the end Justice Kennedy's opposition to any sort, on any scale, of "explicit religious gerrymandering." From either perspective, the Kiryas Joel district marked a step on a dangerous path. Madison again is our guide: "It is proper to take alarm at the first experiment on our liberties."[16]

8

MODESTY AND MUTUAL
RESPECT

WHAT can we hope it may profit us to have taken the partial bird's-eye view of American church-state experience offered in the preceding seven chapters? I undertake here to distill some basic lessons or reminders that might emerge from this effort.

Begin with Learned Hand, one of our immortal jurists, who spoke of the "spirit of liberty" as the "spirit that is not too sure it is right."[1] If we were left with only a single bulwark to preserve our liberties, we would be well advised to vote with Judge Hand for the prevalence of that spirit. No matter how deep your faith, the quality of being "too sure" resides in the disposition to impose it on others. When the First Amendment is working as it should, as it has for the most part, it protects us against that disposition. The greatest lesson of our First Amendment jurisprudence is the virtue of standing fast against the majority's power to veto the claims of freedom—whether by compelling conformity to prevailing sentiments or by giving the state power over religion or permitting any church to acquire some of the state's power.

The spirit that is too sure it's right is spawned by ignorance and fear. The ignorance derives largely from an unawareness of the contingent and accidental nature of our deepest beliefs. Whether your parents were Buddhists, animists, Baptists, Jews, Jehovah's Witnesses, or something else, it is overwhelmingly probable that you are what they are or were. With rare exceptions, we don't make independent selections among the multitude of options. We don't seek out and find for ourselves the true or right religion. It is not necessarily bad that this should be so. The sense of oneness with those who came before and those who will come after is one of the warm mysteries that are inspiring and sustaining.

At the same time, there are indeed the exceptions. The children of atheists recapture the faith of their ancestors or turn to new dispensations. People born to the faith lapse. Some change religions. New religions appear; all the religions of our time had their origins in relatively recent, known, recorded history. One or more of these religions may have the ultimate answers. Or they may not.

The diverse possibilities disclosed by human experience should teach the folly of being too sure you're right. And the willingness to imagine, or even pretend, that one might be wrong is a central premise of the First Amendment. Working against that premise, however, in addition to ignorance, is also the problem of fear, as I've called it, the fear that one's deepest convictions could be questioned or, God forbid, that one's own faith is less than absolutely secure. Reinhold Niebuhr wrote of this:

> Extreme orthodoxy betrays by its very frenzy that the poison of skepticism has entered the soul of the Church;

for men insist most vehemently upon the certainties when their hold upon them has been shaken. Frantic orthodoxy is a method for obscuring doubt.[2]

That species of discomfort, if one has it, must be borne or mastered if the principles of the First Amendment are to be accepted.

Recall Learned Hand again, invoking Oliver Cromwell to expand on the thought quoted at the outset of this chapter:

"I beseech ye in the bowels of Christ, think that ye may be mistaken." I should like to have that written over the portals of every church, every school, and every court house, and, may I say, of every legislative body in the United States. I should like to have every court begin, "I beseech ye in the bowels of Christ, think that we may be mistaken."[3]

On a rational cost-benefit analysis, the benefits of Judge Hand's position overwhelmingly preponderate. Have in mind that the subject is principally ideas and beliefs, and conduct only to the extent that others are not injured. Nobody has suggested that we should tolerate killings or even the refusal to pay taxes on the ground of religious beliefs. The proposal is only that we restrain the admittedly powerful urge to coerce others, when or if we can, into professing beliefs we favor or refraining from openly questioning ours. The cost in self-restraint may be strenuous for many of us. The return, immediately and into what we may hope is a long future, is immense.

Put to one side, if you will, that an unfree society is an unhappy environment for the oppressors as well as for the oppressed. Assuming only the normal ranges of sadism and masochism, the enforcers discover after a while that they are within the same walls that confine the prisoners. It is not a warm or happy relationship. Nor a secure one. Observing the extreme case of the totalitarian state, we count ourselves lucky to move about and speak without the chill of being watched or the chore of doing the surveillance.

The problem of security is of wider importance. It points the way from Hobbes's *Leviathan* (with people forming governments because life in a hypothesized anarchy was nasty, brutish, and short) to the higher state in which we secure freedom by vouchsafing it to each other. It is probably fair in the end, and not cynical, to see that the question may be at bottom one of power. A good many people find it comfortable for now, and sufficient, to extol, and propose to enforce, the values of what they call the Judeo-Christian tradition. Theirs is not a long view. Recall again that Islam is the fastest growing religion. It may or may not come to predominate. We can be nearly certain, however, that the current state of affairs will not endure. Today's Protestant minority in the United States may thank its ancestors who fashioned decent places for minorities when they were a majority. Today's power structure should be preserving that tradition. It is the essence of the Bill of Rights.

The subject of power is not a simple matter of which majority sits on which minority at any given time. Looking around the world today and back through history, we see the horrors to which interreligious conflicts can lead—Muslims versus Hindus, Orthodox Eastern Serbs and Croatian Roman Catholics against Bosnian Muslims, Catholics versus Protestants in much of Europe after the sixteenth century, not to omit our own lesser, but horrible, history of persecutions in colonial America and the martyrdom of Joseph Smith as well as a number of his Mormon followers. We see, too, the fragility of the lessons these oceans of blood should have taught. The powerless call out for tolerance. Achieving power, they may soon forget. The descendants of Rome's Christian martyrs remember too well the role of the torturers rather than the agonies of their own ancestors. Orthodox Jews, who were content just to be let alone in Detroit or Brooklyn, are soon demanding that pork be outlawed and that nobody be allowed to ride buses on the Jewish Sabbath in Israel.

To guard against misunderstanding, I should underscore that the stand against those who are "too sure" they're right is not a plea for skepticism or indifference about matters of religious belief. It is entirely possible to hold your religious beliefs with powerful certainty while not being "too sure" in the sense used here, following Learned Hand and a host of others. As was said at the outset of this chapter, the vice in being *too* sure for our purposes is the disposition to impose your beliefs and your forms of religious conduct on others. That attitude is the enemy of religious freedom. It is the remembered and hated form of oppression against which the First Amendment was drawn.

The pantheon of great figures who have argued against being too sure is made up almost entirely of visibly devout people—including, just for example, Roger Williams, Reinhold Niebuhr, Oliver Cromwell, Tom Paine, and the Justices who voted to exclude prayer from the public schools. The deep purpose, it bears repeating, is to ensure everyone's freedom of conscience and religious practice by making sure, among other things, to keep separate Roger Williams's garden (of religious faith) from the wilderness (of state power). The fundamental protection against those who are too sure is the guarantee that they will be prevented from compelling others to do and believe as they do.

The idea of "tolerance" has had a mixed reception. Through the centuries, embattled minorities have rejected it, construing it to mean condescension and "sufferance." But this conception is not what the First Amendment is about. The assurances of free exercise and that there will be no law respecting an establishment of religion are *rights* that go with being human and being *here*; citizenship is not a requirement for their enjoyment. Nobody can presume to condescend to grant the regime of tolerance commanded by the Constitution. Rights are entitlements that we are all empowered to demand. It is in this sense that our history and our ethos signify tolerance. The meaning is a relationship among equals that includes mutually respectful acceptance of differences.

In a population of which 90 percent or so have never doubted either God's existence or the prospect of life after death, the differences to be respected are usually differences among revealed religions.[4] These do not by and large create serious problems today. There are, to be sure, more instances than we would like of intolerance and harassment—against followers of Islam, Jews, and minority religions like the Santería discussed in Chapter 5. These are reminders that the profoundly civilized decencies inherent in the Bill of Rights must never be taken for granted. The fact remains that the overwhelmingly shared acceptance of traditional monotheistic beliefs has made frictions between revealed religions a relatively minor concern in the contemporary United States.

The picture is different for the minority who question the traditional churches or profess agnosticism or, worse yet, atheism. Even those who believe in God are looked at a little askance when they reject the more or less standard religions. Tom Paine, generally viewed in his late-eighteenth-century world as a dangerous revolutionary, exemplified this position. In a passage written in 1794 (which came to my attention when it was quoted by Justice Stevens in a talk given in 1985), he said:

> I believe in one God, and no more; and I hope for happiness beyond this life.
> I believe in the equality of man; and I believe that religious duties consist in doing justice, loving mercy, and endeavoring to make our fellow creatures happy.
> But, lest it should be supposed that I believe in many other things in addition to these, I shall, in the progress of

this work, declare the things I do not believe, and my reasons for not believing them.

I do not believe in the creed professed by the Jewish church, by the Roman church, by the Greek church, by the Turkish church, by the Protestant church, nor by any church that I know of. My own mind is my own church.

All national institutions of churches, whether Jewish, Christian, or Turkish, appear to me no other than human inventions, set up to terrify and enslave mankind, and monopolize power and profit.

I do not mean by this declaration to condemn those who believe otherwise; they have the same right to their belief as I have to mine. But it is necessary to the happiness of man that he be mentally faithful to himself. Infidelity does not consist in believing or disbelieving; it consists in professing to believe what he does not believe.[5]

Tom Paine's stance, however unpopular with his contemporaries, is not disturbing or offensive to most of us today. Less acceptable even now, however, are the miscellaneous minorities whose fundamental beliefs reject or fail to include the idea of God or gods in accounting for the mysteries of the universe. The varieties of such people range from just left of Tom Paine to the aggressive atheists that John Dewey found philosophically indistinguishable from the most devout supernaturalists we usually think of as lodged at the opposite end of the spectrum. In its treatment of these diversities, the law has, as usual, tended toward the ideological center of gravity. The genuinely respectable norm is represented by "believers." They are contrasted for a number of purposes with the negative "nonbelievers." Or "religion," as we noted earlier, is contrasted with "nonreligion" or "irreligion." A minority of Justices still remains unreconciled to the prevailing position that the neutrality commanded by the Religion Clauses prevails not only between religions but between religion and nonreligion, as it is said.

The goal of complete neutrality, in the nature of the matter, is still a little visionary, and is perhaps unattainable. For example, Congress has for a long time granted conscientious exemptions from combat for draftees opposed to war by reason of "religious training and belief," but not for those philosophically opposed in terms of a purely personal moral code. The Supreme Court has had some interesting visits with that distinction and has been pressed toward some subtle dialectic in the process. In 1965, dealing with some obviously earnest and thoughtful young men, the Court ruled that the law had to leave room for more than adherents of the traditional religions. It settled on a test that would include a "sincere and meaningful belief which occupies in the life of its possessor a place parallel to that filled by the God of those admittedly qualifying for the exemption."[6] In justifying its view of what Congress could fairly have covered in designating "religious" beliefs, the Court found it necessary to cope not only with standard legal materials but with a range of theological writings dealing with the conception of God and sketching "the broad spectrum of religious beliefs found among us."

Five years later another registrant pushed the Court somewhat harder. Elliott Ashton Welsh II had been convicted for unlawfully refusing induction. In carefully written papers claiming conscientious objector status, he had refused to define his training or belief as "religious" and had been unable either to affirm or deny a belief in a Supreme Being. As the Supreme Court observed in the course of reversing his conviction, there was no question that Welsh sincerely believed war to be "wrong, unethical, and immoral," or that his conscience "forbade [him] to take part in such an evil practice."[7] The Court held it made no difference that Welsh had rejected the adjective "religious" to define his beliefs. It was enough, Justice Black wrote, that he held his philosophical beliefs "with the strength of more traditional religious convictions," concluding that the law should be read to exempt "all those whose consciences, spurred by deeply held moral, ethical, *or* religious beliefs, would give them no rest or peace if they allowed themselves to become a part of an instrument of war."[8]

The word "or," which I've italicized in that quotation, made a somewhat creative reading of a statute that seemed literally to afford exemptions *only* for "religious training and belief." Justice John Harlan, while joining in reversal of the conviction, found that more of a strain than he could manage. He wanted to face the fact that Congress had indeed distinguished between beliefs that were "religious" (and favored) and "nonreligious" (denied the favor). And that, he concluded, was unconstitutional, violating the Establishment Clause. The statute could be saved, however, in his view, by extending the exemption to the nonreligious, and he joined on that basis in reversing the conviction. Three of the Justices, dissenting, agreed with Harlan that the statute exempted only for "religious" beliefs, but they held that Congress had the power to do this. They would have upheld Welsh's conviction.

The struggle in those conscientious objector cases reflects tensions wider than the ambit of constitutional law. Justice Harlan, writing only for purposes of legal reasoning, expressed wisdom of moment beyond the courthouse:

> The common denominator must be the intensity of moral conviction with which a belief is held. Common experience teaches that among "religious" individuals some are weak and others strong adherents to tenets and this is no less true of individuals whose lives are guided by personal ethical considerations.

If we can one day realize the full implications of the First Amendment and the mutually respectful community of free people, that lesson, well learned, will be part of our spiritual equipment. We will have learned that the sense of the sacred is no monopoly of any group or school or sect.

Both the law and the widespread sentiments of the public are crabbed and simpleminded in distinguishing religion from its absence, as if the minds and hearts of the so-called non-religious were empty of any concern or conception about what the ultimate things might be. Having taken no poll, but merely from being around a long time, I assert with confidence that substantially every sentient and normally intelligent member of a civilized community has some belief or system of beliefs about such matters. It may amount in the end to no more than a helpless but somehow reverent sense of awed ignorance. It may be a somewhat arrogant conviction that it will all come clear when the magical human mind has had time to work it out. Whatever the "nonbelievers" believe, they scarcely fail to run up against the inevitable questions that attend the human condition.

In that vital sense, the standard notions of religion and its antithesis omit much of the real world. Capturing some of the commonly neglected realities, William James pointed to them in the title of his classic work *The Varieties of Religious Experience.*[9] He defined "religion," with italics, broadly enough to include the *"feelings, acts, and experiences of individual men in their solitude, so far as they apprehend themselves to stand in relation to whatever they may consider the divine."* Julian Huxley, eminent biologist and philosopher, who devoted more deep and sensitive thought to the subject than most of us do, came to a conception of "evolutionary humanism" that included centrally the "capacity for awe and reverence" and a "sense of sacredness" that came out of the human "capacity for experiencing sanctity; just as . . . he has for experiencing red or blue, fear or disgust or desire."[10] His rejection of revelation and the supernatural was of course rejected in turn by most of his contemporaries. But the notion of setting him off as a "nonbeliever" is a crass species of philistinism.

Huxley was literally an atheist, still a dirty word for Western majorities. It would be difficult nevertheless to describe him as a villain or a fool. But consult again Father John Courtney Murray, humane and spacious in most respects and unshakably sure of his true religion. Commenting on "Justice Rutledge's echo of the Madisonian theology" and the idea of the First Amendment that every person's sacred religious privacy is to be protected by the wall of separation, Father Murray said: "I take it that atheism is analogously the kingdom of the individual man and his Infinite Blank of Ultimate Doubt or whatever inhabits that kingdom, and has a similar sacredness."[11] One is driven to identify in the noted theologian an acid smugness that resides uneasily with the spirit of the First Amendment and the general spirit of liberty for which Learned Hand spoke. There was never reason to doubt Father Murray's long distance from the Inquisition and Galileo's anguish, but the echoes of his spiritual ancestry were not inaudible.

Recalling the Inquisition is liable to be painful or offensive to someone, but it is nonetheless salubrious on that score. Dostoevsky's Grand Inquisitor may have been an atheist, after all, or simply for his creator the Roman Catholic enemy of Russian Orthodoxy. In the present context, he symbolizes the central role of all inquisitors—as enemies of freedom. It pays for us to remember the likes of the Grand Inquisitor's real-life descendants in the Soviet Union. They, too, scorned the idea of equal treatment for atheism and belief in God. Now that traditional religion has emerged from the underground in Russia, we would be fools to forget that the spirit too sure of its rightness may not always favor us, whoever we are.

Fortunately, despite the appearance of petty inquisitors from time to time, the pressure for orthodoxy in religious conceptions has never prevailed in America. There can be no heresy here. Or blasphemy. We are all free to believe as we please. And none of us is entitled to force beliefs on others. Above all, no person and no church is brigaded with the power of the state or condemned to be coerced by the state in matters of conscience.

An inheritance that includes these principles is priceless. We owe ourselves and our posterity the duty to preserve it.

NOTES

CHAPTER 1

1. 330 U.S. 1 (1947).
2. Ibid., p. 16.
3. Ibid., p. 18.
4. Ibid., p. 19.
5. Ibid., p. 24.
6. Ibid., p. 29.
7. Ibid., p. 31.
8. Ibid., p. 53.
9. Ibid., p. 63.
10. 112 S.Ct. at 2685.
11. 465 U.S. 668 (1984).
12. *Allegheny County v. Greater Pittsburgh ACLU*, 492 U.S. 573, 578–79 (1989).

13. Quoted by Justice Douglas in the foreword to *The Bible and the Schools* (Boston, Mass: Little, Brown, 1966).

CHAPTER 2

1. Donna E. Arzt, *Religious Freedom in a Religious State: The Case of Israel in Comparative Constitutional Perspective*, 9 Wis. Int'l L.J. 1, 10 (1990).
2. *Writings of James Madison* 184, 186, 188, 189 (Hunt ed., New York: G. P. Putnam, 1901–10).
3. *See* A. Stokes and L. Pfeffer, *Church and State in the United States* (New York: Harper & Row, 1964), 23–24.
4. Wilbur K. Jordan, *The Development of Religious Toleration in England* (Cambridge, Mass.: Harvard University Press, 1940), 475.
5. José Ortega y Gasset, *The Revolt of the Masses* (New York: W. W. Norton, 1932), 83.

CHAPTER 3

1. Robert T. Handy, *A Christian America: Protestant Hope and Historical Realities* viii (New York: Oxford University Press, 1971).
2. *Id.* at 216.
3. *Peoples v. Ruggles*, 8 Johns 290, 295 (N.Y., 1811).
4. *Vidal v. Girard's Executors*, 43 U.S. (2 How.) 127, 198 (1844).
5. *Church of Jesus Christ of Latter-Day Saints v. United States*, 136 U.S. 1, 49 (1890).
6. *Holy Trinity Church v. United States*, 143 U.S. 457, 470–71 (1892).
7. *U.S. v. Macintosh*, 283 U.S. 605, 625 (1931).
8. *Lynch v. Donnelly*, 465 U.S. 668, 718 (1984) (dissenting opinion).
9. *R. v. Chief Metropolitan Stipendiary Magistrate* [1991] 1 QB 429.
10. *Commonwealth v. Cooke*, 7 Am. L. Reg. 417 (Mass Police Ct., 1850).

11. *Donahue v. Richards*, 38 Maine 379 (1854).
12. *Engel v. Vitale*, 370 U.S. 421 (1962).
13. Stokes and Pfeffer, op. cit., 378–79.
14. *The Writings of James Madison*, op. cit., 132 n.3.
15. Douglas, op. cit., 40.
16. *Engel v. Vitale*, 370 U.S. 421 (1962).
17. Erwin Griswold, *Absolute Is in the Dark*, 8 Utah L. Rev. 167, 176 (1963).
18. *American Jewish Congress v. City of Chicago*, No. 85 C. 9471, slip op. at 10 (N.D., Ill., Nov. 5, 1986).
19. 827 F.2d 120 (7th Cir. 1987).
20. 112 S. Ct. at 2685.
21. *Id.* at 2686.
22. David Hume, *Of the Parties of Great Britain*, in *David Hume's Political Essays* (C. Hendel ed., New York: Liberal Arts Press, 1953), 86.
23. H.L.A. Hart, book review, *New York Review of Books*, July 17, 1986, p. 52.
24. John Dewey, *A Common Faith* (New Haven, Conn.: Yale University Press, 1934), 52.

CHAPTER 4

1. *Engel v. Vitale*, 370 U.S. 421 (1962).
2. *Abington School District v. Schempp*, 374 U.S. 203 (1963).
3. *Wallace v. Jaffree*, 472 U.S. 38 (1985).
4. P. 43.
5. *May v. Cooperman*, 572 F. Supp. 1561, 1564 (D. N.J., 1983).
6. *Marsh v. Chambers*, 463 U.S. 783, 792 (1983).
7. *Walter v. West Virginia Bd. of Educ.*, 610 F. Supp. 1169 (D. W.Va. 1985).
8. Tr. 19–25.
9. P. 1173.
10. P. 1178.
11. Douglas Laycock, *Equal Access and Moments of Silence: The Equal Status of Religious Speech by Private Speakers*, 81 Nw.U.L.Rev. 1, 6 (1986).

12. *E.g.*, *Gaines v. Anderson*, 421 F. Supp. 337, 340, 345 (D. Mass., 1976).

13. Matthew 6:1.

14. Quoted in Stokes & Pfeffer, op. cit., 569.

15. Mark Howe, *The Garden and the Wilderness* (Chicago: University of Chicago Press, 1965), 175.

16. *Aronow v. United States*, 432 F.2d 242, 243 (9th Cir. 1970).

17. H.R. Rep. No. 1693, 83rd Cong., 2d Sess. (1954).

18. 100 Cong. Rec. 7757–66, 7833–34 (1954).

19. Leonid Feldman, in David Dalin, ed., *American Jews & the Separationist Faith* (Washington, D.C.: Ethics and Public Policy Center, 1993), 44–45.

20. *Board of Trustees of the Village of Scarsdale v. McCreary*, 471 U.S. 83 (1985).

21. *John Doe v. Duncanville Independent School District*, 986 F.2d 953 (5th Cir., 1993).

22. P. 261.

23. Pp. 81–82.

24. George Marsden, "A Case of the Excluded Middle: Creation versus Evolution in America," in Robert Bellah and Frederick Greenspan, *Uncivil Religion* (New York: Crossroad, 1987), 132, 143.

25. Alexis de Toqueville, *Democracy in America* (Phillips Bradley, ed., New York: Vintage Books, 1945), 319–26.

CHAPTER 5

1. *Torcaso v. Watkins*, 367 U.S. 488 (1961).

2. *Minersville School District v. Gobitis*, 310 U.S. 586 (1940), overruled in *West Virginia Board of Education v. Barnette*, 319 U.S. 624 (1943).

3. *Wooley v. Maynard*, 430 U.S. 705 (1977).

4. Quoted 367 U.S. at 494 n.9.

5. *Reynolds v. United States*, 98 U.S. 145, 164 (1879).

6. *Id.*

7. Pp. 166–67.

8. *Prince v. Massachusetts*, 321 U.S. 158 (1944).

9. P. 176.
10. *Wisconsin v. Yoder*, 406 U.S. 205 (1972).
11. P. 209.
12. P. 210.
13. *Id.*
14. *Id.*
15. P. 215.
16. P. 247.
17. *Sherbert v. Verner*, 374 U.S. 398 (1963).
18. *Braunfeld v. Brown*, 366 U.S. 599 (1961).
19. *Estate of Thornton v. Caldor, Inc.*, 472 U.S. 703 (1985).
20. 494 U.S. 872.
21. Oregon Revised Statutes § 475.992(5)(a)&(b) (1991).
22. *Church of the Lukumi Babalu Aye v. City of Hialeah*, 113 S.Ct. 2217 (1993).

CHAPTER 6

1. *West Virginia Board of Education v. Barnette*, 319 U.S. 624, 642 (1943).
2. 322 U.S. 78.
3. *Id.* at 86–87.
4. *United States v. Bakker*, 925 F.2d 728, 731 (4th Cir., 1991).
5. *United States v. Moon*, 718 F.2d 1210, 1216 (2d Cir., 1983), *cert. denied*, 466 U.S. 971 (1984).
6. *Ran-Dav's County Kosher v. State*, 129 N.J. 141 (1992).

CHAPTER 7

1. *We Hold These Truths—Catholic Reflections on the American Proposition* (Kansas City, Mo.: Sheed and Ward, 1960), 145, 148.
2. "Law or Prepossessions?," 14 *Law and Contemporary Problems* 23, 25, 31 (1949).
3. *Board of Education v. Allen*, 392 U.S. 236 (1968).
4. *McCollum v. Board of Education*, 333 U.S. 203 (1948).
5. *Zorach v. Clauson*, 343 U.S. 306 (1952).

6. *School District of Grand Rapids v. Ball*, 473 U.S. 373 (1985); *Meek v. Pittenger*, 421 U.S. 349 (1975).
7. *Wolman v. Walter*, 433 U.S. 229 (1977).
8. *Committee for Public Education v. Nyquist*, 413 U.S. 756 (1973).
9. *Mueller v. Allen*, 463 U.S. 388 (1983).
10. *Zobrest v. Catalina Foothills School District*, 113 S.Ct. 2462 (1993).
11. *Grand Rapids* case, *supra*, 473 U.S. at 395.
12. *Board of Education of Kiryas Joel v. Grumet*, 114 S.Ct. 2481 (1994).
13. The quoted words are Professor Joseph Goldstein's, making this complaint in a nice book, *The Intelligible Constitution* (New York and Oxford: Oxford University Press, 1992).
14. *N.Y. Times*, June 29, 1994, p. A22.
15. *Meek v. Pittenger*, 421 U.S. 349, 372 (1975).
16. "Memorial and Remonstrance against Religious Assessments," quoted in dissent of Rutledge, J., in *Everson v. Board of Education*, 330 U.S. at 65 (1947).

CHAPTER 8

1. "The Spirit of Liberty" in the book of essays by that name, (New York: Alfred A. Knopf, 1952), 190.
2. *Does Civilization Need Religion?*, 2–3 (1927).
3. "Morals in Public Life," in *The Spirit of Liberty*, 229–30 (1952).
4. See, e.g., Garry Wills, *Under God: Religion and American Politics* (1991).
5. *The Age of Reason*, 304 (Bobbs-Merrill, 1948).
6. *United States v. Seeger*, 380 U.S. 163, 176 (1965).
7. *Welsh v. United States*, 398 U.S. 333, 337 (1970).
8. *Id.* at 343–44.
9. Modern Library ed., 1902.
10. *Religion without Revelation* (New York: New American Library, 1957), 98, 102–4, 111, 188, 190.
11. "Law or Prepossessions?," at 30–31 and note 30.

SELECTED

BUT DIVERSE

BIBLIOGRAPHY

1. Arlin M. Adams and Charles J. Emmerich. *A Nation Dedicated to Religious Liberty* (Philadelphia: University of Pennsylvania Press, 1990)
2. Thomas J. Curry. *The First Freedoms: Church and State in America and the Passing of the First Amendment* (New York: Oxford University Press, 1986)
3. Mark de Wolfe Howe. *The Garden and the Wilderness* (University of Chicago Press, 1965)
4. Philip B. Kurland. *Religion and the Law* (Chicago: Aldine, 1961)
5. Leonard W. Levy. *The Establishment Clause* (New York: Macmillan, 1986)
6. William Lee Miller. *The First Liberty* (New York: Alfred A. Knopf, 1986)
7. Anson Phelps Stokes. *Church and State in the United States* (New York: Harper Bros., 1950)

INDEX